BEN RANDALL

A CATECHISM ON THE THIRTY-NINE ARTICLES OF RELIGION

INTRO DUCING ANGLICA NISM

WestBow Press books may be ordered through booksellers or by contacting:

WestBow Press
A Division of Thomas Nelson & Zondervan
1663 Liberty Drive
Bloomington, IN 47403
www.westbowpress.com
844-714-3454

The text of the "Thirty-Nine Articles" is taken from: *The Book of Common Prayer and Administration of the Sacraments and Other Rites and Ceremonies of the Church together with The Psalter or Psalms of David According to the use of The Episcopal Church.* New York, NY: Church Publishing Inc., 2007.

New International Reader's Version (NIRV)
Copyright © 1995, 1996, 1998, 2014 by Biblica, Inc.®. Used by permission. All rights reserved worldwide.

Interior Watercolor Artist: Lynn French-Mumford

ISBN: 979-8-3850-1743-0 (sc)
ISBN: 979-8-3850-1744-7 (hc)
ISBN: 979-8-3850-1745-4 (e)

Library of Congress Control Number: 2024901454

Print information available on the last page.

WestBow Press rev. date: 09/18/2024

WESTBOW
PRESS®
A DIVISION OF THOMAS NELSON
& ZONDERVAN

AUTHOR'S PREFACE FOR THE COURSE-LEADER

Jesus said, '"I am the way the truth and the life"' (Jn 14:6). This means that the content of our beliefs (our 'doctrine'), the kind of people we are (our characters), and whether we will eventually enjoy eternity with Jesus, are tightly intertwined; they're inseparable. Basically, that's the impetus behind this course on the Thirty-Nine Articles of Religion.

Hello! I'm Father Ben, a priest ordained in the Church of England currently serving in the United States. I never planned to make this contribution to the already saturated space of discipling young Christians. However, during the online classes I was forced to adopt at the beginning of the COVID pandemic, it became uncomfortably clear that the candidates in my congregation who I had begun to prepare for confirmation knew somewhat the stories of Holy Scripture, but often hadn't deeply absorbed the ideas therein—those ideas that are supposed to shape us into men and women after the Lord's own heart. Certainly, the few ideas or 'theology' that they had acquired were far too thin to form anything like a 'worldview', especially not an *Anglican* one. Yet how could we blame them? Often those of us serious about the Bible and sincerely believing its inspiration, have, in this tradition, for our children, grabbed a little bit of 'this' and a little bit of 'that' from the curricula of confessionally-Calvinist, nondenominational, or Roman Catholic organizations. We haven't been serious about the treasures *we* boast. No wonder, then, that our youngest members often 'drift' to other fellowships and expressions—*if they remain faithful at all,* of course!

So, how should you run this course—if you're choosing to use this book in that way? The formula is simple: purchase a copy for yourself and one for every individual who will be engaging in this study with you. Each student needs their own because they will be required, here and there, to write and draw in the pages that follow.

There isn't much prep for you as leader. That's good news, right? I assume you're a busy person on a tight schedule. I also assume you might be a volunteer, and I want you to know that I respect, and am grateful for, the commitment you're making. Just do your best to read the session to yourself beforehand. Grab some pens and at least one Bible. I recommend the *New International Reader's Version*. It might be helpful to highlight any of the quoted scriptures *before* a session gets underway. In fact, I'd encourage you to do that, and then to open the Bible to show the highlighted passages when the occasion arises, even if just with a casual flourish.

Once your group has gathered and you're ready to begin, whoever is taking the lead on teaching simply needs to read the text aloud, pausing here and there as necessary to clarify concepts or answer questions. However, I'd ask you to trust that something complex or difficult will be restated, revisited, and reinforced in the next paragraph, over the page, or in a later session. You might find yourself saying *ad nauseam*, "Let's see if Father Ben explains that in a moment," or similar.

Don't forget: enthusiasm is infectious. If *you* evidently love Christ, they'll be curious as to why. If *you* think belonging to any of the branches of the (fractured) Anglican Communion is awesome, so will they. On the other hand, if your attitude is "Meh," then expect to fail. Success, by the way, does not mean that every individual who engages with this course walks away having memorized verbatim the Articles. No. Rather, success is knowing better why the Gospel—the so-called 'Good News'—is *great* news. They should also have a deeper appreciation of God's holiness, a firmer conviction that Christ died for them, and that this is a transformative truth, which touches every aspect of who we are.

God bless you.

CONTENTS

THE WATERCOLORS

SESSION 1

Foreword
Why Are We Here?

Now *there's* a question! Is it because of millions of random chemical reactions? Is it because our ancestors were "the fittest"? Is it because a monkey-like creature in East Africa figured out one day, long ago, how to put a *really* sharp edge on a piece of flint, and so rose to the top of the food chain? Suddenly all the extra meat in that monkey-like creature's diet meant it grew the biggest brain of all the animals, and invented crop-rotation, Chick-fil-a, and TikTok? Or is it because you went backward in time in a modified DeLorean and punched your dad's high-school nemesis in the face who *would* have taken your mom to the prom, and so your dad took her dancing instead and they fell in love and—oh, wait! That last one is a movie called *Back to the Future*. Check it out.

No, let's be more specific. For what reason have you this particular book in hand? Simple: to discover for ourselves this thing called the "Thirty-Nine Articles of Religion." And, in so doing, come, I hope, to understand the Bible much, much better. But why does *that* matter? Well, during the coronation of King Charles III (of England), the Archbishop of Canterbury—the man who actually put the crown on Charles' head—handed him a Bible, saying that it was "*the* most valuable thing that this world affords."[1] *Wow!* But do *you* believe that? Do you believe that the Bible is *the* most "valuable thing"? What about money? Or being famous? Or beauty? Or your health?

---

[1] "Archbishop of Canterbury Receives the Coronation Bible at Lambeth Palace," *The Archbishop of Canterbury*, posted April 20, 2023, https://www.archbishopofcanterbury.org/news/news-and-statements/archbishop-canterbury-receives-coronation-bible-lambeth-palace#:~:text=When%20the%201953%20Coronation%20Bible,the%20lively%20Oracles%20of%20God.%E2%80%9D. (a.k.a., 'the Eucharist' or 'Holy Communion')

I (Father Ben) believe that the Thirty-Nine Articles help us understand God, ourselves, and the world better. That is to say, they are a really useful tool for helping people understand what *Christians* believe. The course in the book you have in front of you is designed, in particular, for young men and women who have already begun to think of themselves as Christian and want to take the next step in their relationship with Jesus by being confirmed and/or taking Communion for the first time.

Now, if you've never had Communion, you might be wondering, "Why not? Why has it been withheld? What's so special about it? Why doesn't the Church give those little white wafers and sips of wine to everyone? To the ducks swimming on the pond even, and to the squirrels in my yard?" Well, this is just one of lots of important questions we need to think about. After all, you've probably already seen how, for many others in the Church, this strange 'meal' is a powerful, even *emotional*, experience. And, over the many centuries that Christians have being sharing it on Sundays and on other feast-days, usually making it the centrepiece of their worship, they've argued and, tragically, even *killed* each other, because it was understood to be so special—that it was *sacred*.

Something Christians do that is sacred is called a *sacrament*. For many of us Anglicans or Episcopalians (those are basically the same thing, by the way), the first sacrament we received was that of Baptism when we were babies. In other words, we didn't choose for it to happen. It was done *to* us. (And we probably cried and complained the whole time, right?) Being confirmed, however, and eating the Lord's Supper (a.k.a., 'the Eucharist' or 'Holy Communion') is something *you* must decide to do. It's a big deal, like getting married, or choosing a college, or buying your first home. Really, it is. So, let's pray:

LORD God, heavenly Father, we ask that you would send your Holy Spirit to give us wisdom, patience, and gratitude as we learn about the gift of the Thirty-Nine Articles. In Jesus's name we pray, Amen.

What is 'confirmation'? To be 'confirmed' is to declare, in the presence of the bishop and before a congregation—your local church-family, that you want to follow and obey Jesus; that, from now on, when others see you at worship it isn't because your parents or someone else—maybe a spouse—insisted that you come along, but because you chose to show up; because you believe you ought to 'make a [regular] sacrifice of thanksgiving and praise.' (Historically, often, this declaration was made at a special service where the confirmed person took Communion for the first time.) Your Confirmation will be _____.

Introduction
Part 1: Truth and Revelation

A true statement (something I say or write) is one that reflects the reality of things: For example, giraffes have long necks. Birds have wings. Crocodiles have sharp teeth. Those are all true statements. When it comes to making statements about God, however, it can be harder to know what is true or false. Why? Because He's invisible or, as Jesus put it, "God is spirit" (Jn 4:24). This means He doesn't have a physical, observable body like you and me. If we can't see Him, then, how can we know anything about what He's like, His character, what brings Him pleasure, or what makes Him sad or angry? This is a very important question because many people make many different religious claims. Even Christians don't all agree. Some, for instance, say, "God doesn't care if I belong to a worshipping congregation." Others say, "Yes, He does!"

Complete the diagram below, drawing arrows to indicate those statements that you think are true, those that are false, and those that we just don't know.

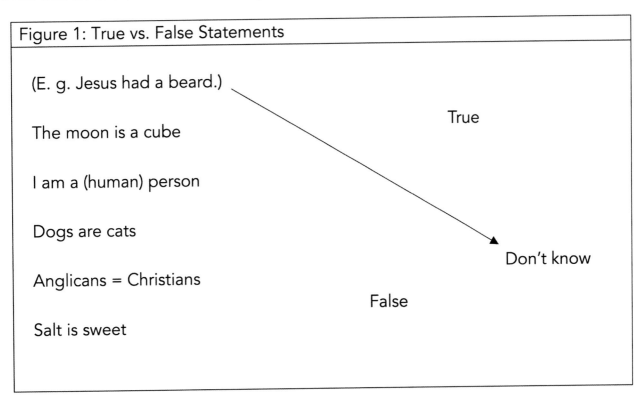

Figure 1: True vs. False Statements

(E. g. Jesus had a beard.)

The moon is a cube

I am a (human) person

Dogs are cats

Anglicans = Christians

Salt is sweet

True

Don't know

False

Well, the Church teaches that God reveals (shows us) what is true about Himself in two ways.

1. General Revelation. What's that? Well, when we look around at the world, we see that certain things are generally true about it: it is beautiful, for example. Think about the wildflowers in

a field, or the colors of a tropical fish. It is also extremely complex: just take a look under a microscope at a hair from your head, or look at a fly's eye or a gemstone. The natural world is also very predictable. There are patterns and rhythms of cause and effect, which we learn to depend upon as human beings, like the rising of the sun in the morning; that spring always follows winter, and so on. In other words, we can learn quite a bit about God from looking at what He has made: that He likes orderliness, for example, and variety.

Do you know what 'entomology' is? It is the study of "critters"—*bugs*. Well, the famous British-Indian entomologist John Haldane was once asked what he thought we could learn about God from insects. After pausing awhile to reflect, he replied, "That He must have an inordinate fondness for beetles." (*Inordinate* means lots and lots.) Why? Why did Haldane think God must like beetles so much? Because there's so many of them: big ones, small ones, some with wings, some with horns, some that jump, some that bite—*urgh!*

However, nature can only tell us so much; it also leaves us guessing at some gaps.

2. Special Revelation fills in the gaps, some of which are huge; others are frightening.* Special revelation are those truths that He, God, was proactive to tell us about in particular. In other words, it is those things about Himself that He has made a 'special' effort to communicate. He didn't just *hope* we would come to understand these realities as we observed and measured His creation (as scientists do). No, special revelation was *directly* communicated to us.

* Why "frightening"? Well, when I look around, I see lots of wonderful and interesting things, yes, but also *death*. Maybe you've lost someone like a grandparent, or a dog? There's so much death everywhere, and that *might*, with some reason, lead me to think that God must like it. So, does He like death? No. This is why He has a plan to (eventually) destroy it. But knowledge of this plan can only be found in *one* place: the Bible.

Let me put it like this. Imagine I'm sitting at a table with you. Suddenly, I take from my bag an orange and place it near to you on (what looks like) "your" side of the table. I do so without saying anything, in silence. What would you think if I did that? Go on—guess.

Answer:

_____

_____

_____

You might think that I wanted you to eat the orange, right? However, you can't be *certain*. After all, maybe where I come from handing fruit to a stranger is a declaration of war against that person: "*Argh...charge!*" Maybe I just want you to admire its waxy, shiny skin and zesty smell. You just don't know unless I *tell* you: "Here, have my orange; it's a gift."

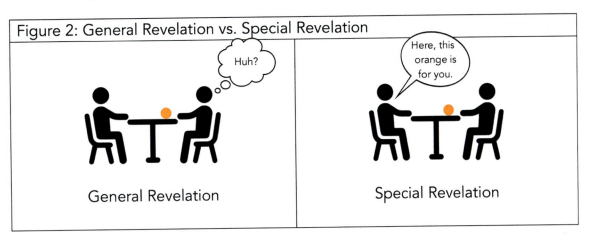

Figure 2: General Revelation vs. Special Revelation

Christians believe that the chosen method of special revelation has been by the Holy Scriptures, i.e., the Bible, which we've already mentioned. This is why, usually, during traditional worship at the end of a reading, you may hear it described as, "The word of the LORD." Because that's what it is! —words "breathed" from His "mouth" (2 Tim 3:16) and shared with us by prophets like Amos; by ancient Jewish leaders like Moses (such as in the book of Deuteronomy); and by apostles like Paul (*Romans* and *Galatians*, among others), and John (the *Gospel of John*, *Revelation*, and so on).

Sometimes, though, it is still hard to know what exactly God is trying to say, which is just one of the many, *many* benefits of Him sending His son, our Savior, to be, as the "beloved Disciple" called Him, "*the* Word" (Jn 1:1). That means the *final* word—to explain and resolve some lingering misunderstanding from the Old Testament, which divided the Jewish people into polarized interpretative-groups in first-century Judea-Syria. That's the time and the place when Jesus was on the Earth. Can you name any of those groups? (Hint: some of them gave Jesus a *very* hard time.)

Answer:

The Essenes

SESSION 2

Introduction
Part 2: The Articles of Religion

Have you ever made a shopping list? Or seen someone else make one? Why? Because it can be difficult to remember all those things that you want to buy on a single, weekly trip for groceries, e.g., milk, sugar, cereal, bacon, soap, rice, and so on.

A shopping list doesn't include everything you need, however, such as air in your lungs and love from your parents. That's not the point of it. Its theme or purpose is a narrow one. Specifically, it is for those things that are needed in the home until the next time you visit the store, which you trust will still be there when you visit again. In the Anglican churches, such as the Church of England, for example, or the one in the United States of America called the Episcopal Church, we have a 'shopping list' of thirty-nine true statements about God. The theme of these is what "[we] believe the Scripture to teach of essential importance, and that…should be held and taught by *all* Christians"[2] In other words, they express what those of us in *this* church tradition think is *correct* theology. *Theology*, by the way, is from Greek; it means "words about God."

Now, the Thirty-Nine Articles are quite old, and there used to be more—forty-two, in fact. Some were tested for a while and found to be confusing and not always helpful. The rest were kept because, when we carefully compare them with what the Bible teaches *as a whole*, balancing the "special revelation" contained in both of its Testaments, we find what seems like a very good match.

The person we have to thank for the Thirty-Nine Articles is one man in particular: a clever, evangelical priest named Thomas Cranmer. (That's his portrait on the front-cover, by the way.) He was the Archbishop of Canterbury under both King Henry VIII of England and Henry's only son, Edward VI, in the sixteenth century. That's about five hundred years ago!

Like most other Englishmen at that time, Cranmer had been a Roman Catholic Christian. With God's help, however, he came to realize that many of the things he had been taught (in occasional sermons from the pulpit and in lectures at college) were *not* very good theology. To fix the situation, he carefully studied the Bible for himself. Then, with some close friends like Peter Martyr Vermigli from Italy, Cranmer wrote a *Book of Common Prayer* to be used throughout the whole kingdom, including, eventually, in her colonies in the New World (of America). In this *Book*, he listed the "Articles."* This is why we're going to learn them together, because right thinking leads to right action.

---

[2] John H. Rodgers, *Essential Truths for Christians: A Commentary on the Anglican Thirty-Nine Articles and an Introduction to Systematic Theology* (Blue Bell, PA: Classical Anglican Press, 2011), 1. (My emphasis.)

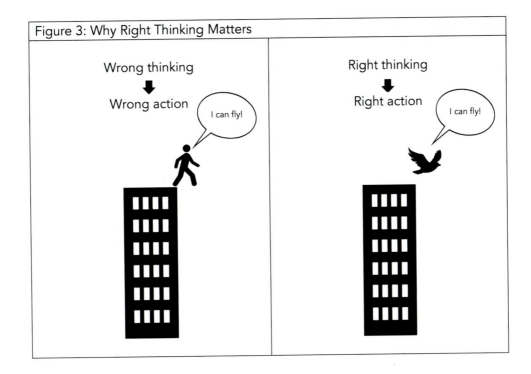

Figure 3: Why Right Thinking Matters

Let me explain the importance of the Articles another way. Jesus said, "'The only way to get to the Father'"—by which He meant to have abundant life with Him (God), including life *after* death(!)—"'is through me.'" (Jn 14:6) We must, then, try as hard as we can to learn who Jesus is, and what He expects from us: the only thing; the only *animal* made "in His"—the Father's—"likeness" (Gen 1:26–27). Our hope to live again—to be *'saved'*—depends on it. That's His claim. That's why He came.

Today, sadly, many doubt that what you believe (your 'religion') could be of such enormous significance. Cranmer, however, knew better. That's why, when Queen Mary I, also known as 'Bloody Mary', threatened to kill him if he didn't change his mind, he refused! He quoted the first martyr, Saint Stephen, saying, "'Lord Jesus, receive my spirit'" (*Acts* 7:59). Thus, on March 21st, 1556, Cranmer was tied to a wooden pole in the town-square of the city of Oxford and set on fire— *murdered*. And many people watched!

Mary had hoped that by doing this to him, and to his friends, she could bully the people of England into staying Roman Catholic. It had the opposite effect. After all, "'If you obey my teaching,' [Jesus] said, 'you are *really* my disciples. Then you will know the truth. And the truth will set you free.'" (See Jn 8:31–32).

* For example, you can find them on pages 867–876 of the American Episcopal Church's *Book of Common Prayer* (1979).

SESSION 3

Article I
Of Faith in the Holy Trinity

There is but one living and true God, everlasting, without body, parts, or passions;
of infinite power, wisdom, and goodness; the maker, and preserver of all things
both visible and invisible. And in unity of this Godhead there be three persons, of
one substance, power, and eternity; the Father, the Son, and the Holy Ghost.

The first and most important Article reminds us of something that most of us on this course probably take for granted: that there *is* a God; He made everything (without help from anyone else); and, He wasn't Himself made. What else do we learn? Cranmer lays out for us six further true statements according to the Bible.

1. God is everlasting, which means He has no end.
2. God is good. In fact, that's where we get the word ("go(o)d") from! We just added an extra "o."
3. He's wise; He sees and understands *everything.*
4. He's powerful! There's *nothing* He can't do.
5. He uses this "power" to keep the universe going. (Your next breath? God allowed it to happen, and He needn't have! *Gulp.*)
6. Finally, the most distinctive or unusual thing about the *Christian* teaching about God is that although there is only *one* of Him, He consists of three *different* persons.

This last one is something that most of us struggle to understand, and with good reason. In our experience, such a thing is impossible: we are each one mind in a single body; when I look inside, I just find myself there. Just close your eyes and try it.

(Pause.)

Was there someone else looking back at you? No, but God is…different, more interesting. I wonder, do you know any of the names we've given to God's persons?

Answer:

The Son
_____   _____   _____

In Ireland many years ago, Saint Patrick compared God's trinitarianism (that's the proper word for His three-in-oneness, by the way), to a shamrock, a clover-leaf. I (that is, Father Ben) sometimes say, a bit jokingly, that God is similar to Ghidorah, the enemy of the Japanese lizard-giant, Godzilla:

In the movie, Ghidorah has *three* heads; and, presumably, each of those heads has a private, interior life. —its own thoughts, feelings, dreams, etc. Indeed, Ghidorah's heads might not even like each other! Maybe they squabble and fight. But those heads aren't separable individuals; they would wither and die if they were somehow severed from the body. Yes, *one* head *isn't* Ghidorah *by itself;* only a part of it. No, *all* of Ghidorah, undivided and intact, is really Ghidorah. And God is a little like this, except that He has no parts that can be removed: If I invited, let's say, the Father into a room with me, I can't suddenly slam the door shut leaving one or two of His other persons standing outside. They are always *everywhere* together. Isn't that weird? —It's okay to say, "yes." But it's also an essential part of why He's wonderful! Thus sang the psalmist in the Bible, thousands of years ago:

Who up there in the skies above
can compare with the Lord?
Not the stars or the planets.
And who among the angels is like Him?
God is highly respected…
He's more wonderful than *all* those
who circle around Him. (89:5–7)

Amen?*

* *Amen* is a strange word. It means "I agree" or "*agreed*." So, do you? Notice the question mark. I'm asking, "Do you think God is more fascinating and greater than anything else in the universe?" If you think yes, then say, "Amen."

Article II
Of the Word or Son of God, Which Was Made Very Man

The Son, which is the Word of the Father, begotten from everlasting of the Father, the very and eternal God, and of one substance with the Father, took Man's nature in the womb of the blessed Virgin, of her substance: so that two whole and perfect Natures, that is to say, the Godhead and Manhood, were joined together in one Person, never to be divided, whereof is one Christ, very God, and very Man; who truly suffered, was crucified, dead, and buried, to reconcile his Father to us, and to be a sacrifice, not only for original guilt, but also for all actual sins of men.

God is, then, three persons, and one of those persons is called "the Son." His human name was—yup, you guessed it—*Jesus.*

Jesus was born in Bethlehem, lived in Nazareth, and died in Jerusalem—all cities in the country that today is called Israel (at the eastern edge of the Mediterranean Sea). He was tempted by the Devil, He was a miracle worker who could control the weather and walk on water, and He was a healer of incurable diseases. He did many, many incredible things; things that aroused the curiosity of those who saw them: "Who on earth *is* this guy? A wizard? An alien?"

Jesus's answer was audacious: "'I and the Father are one'" (Jn 10:30). But how?! How can Jesus be both God the Creator *and* one of God's (human) creatures? Truthfully, it is impossible for us to fully understand the mystery of God with our brains. In fact, trying to do so is a bit like trying to pour all the world's oceans—the Atlantic, the Pacific, and the others—into a single, regular teacup. It just can't be done, right? Enough seawater *does* fit, however, so that we can get an accurate sense of its saltiness, for example.

Well, some very clever men and women have, over the years, successfully found ways to describe fundamental truths about God. One such person was 'Tertullian'. He was a Berber, indigenous to North Africa; he spoke both Greek and Latin fluently. And he used his extraordinary gifts to explain to his pagan neighbors (in the 2nd c.) why Christianity is a *reasonable* religion, more plausible than *any* other, especially more so than their traditional ideas about Jupiter, Mars, Venus, and so on.

Tertullian not only invented the word 'Trinity', *he* said that Jesus possessed *two* "substances": "in one respect born, in the other unborn; in one respect fleshly, in the other spiritual; in one sense weak, in the other exceeding strong; in one sense [ageing and] dying, in the other [continually] living."[3] These substances coexist (side-by-side) in Christ somehow to make His "*hypostasis*"—a one-of-a-kind union:

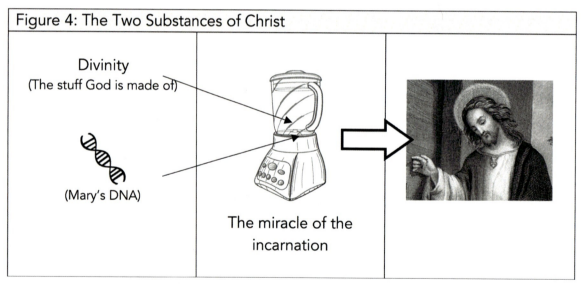

Figure 4: The Two Substances of Christ

Divinity
(The stuff God is made of)

(Mary's DNA)

The miracle of the incarnation

Of course, I don't need to tell you Jesus wasn't *actually* made in a food blender but rather in the womb of the blessed virgin, Mary. It was the most wonderful miracle *ever*, and to illustrate the mystery of it, try the activity on the next page. (You're going to need some paint…)

---

[3] Tertullian, "On the Flesh of Christ," *Christian Classics Ethereal Library*, accessed November 7, 2023, https://ccel.org/ccel/tertullian/christ_flesh/anf03.v.vii.i.html.

Figure 5: The "Hypostasis" of Christ		
The "substance" of God: DIVINITY	The "substance" of a human: HUMANITY	The "hypostasis" of Christ: SAVIOR
G	(figure)	(figure with halo)
 +	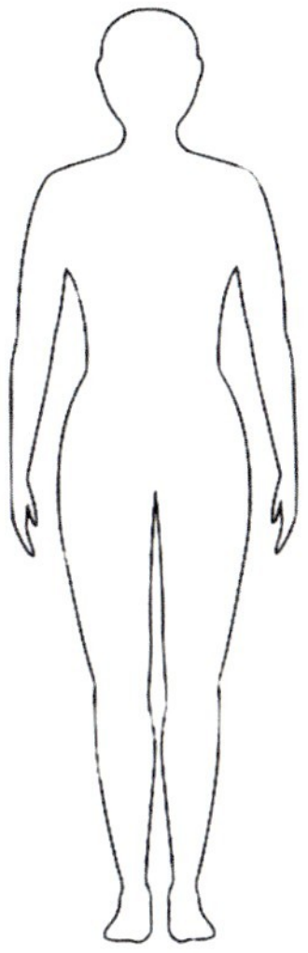 =	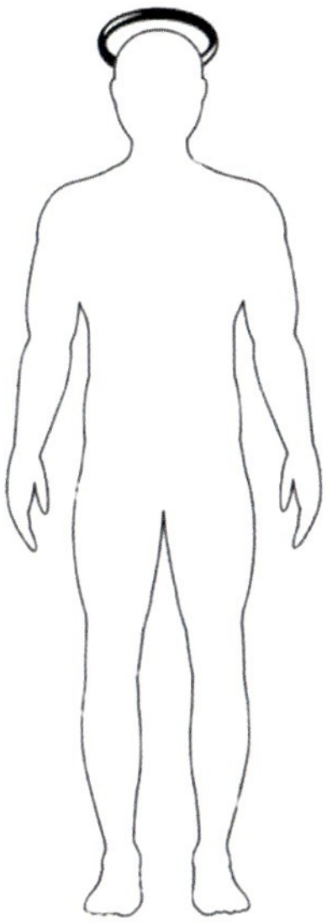
Pour out some blue paint; then, with a brush, color the "G."	Pour out some red paint; then, with a brush, apply it to the figure above.	Now, mix the remainder of the blue AND red paints <u>together</u>, and then apply it here ↲.

Now, it may seem like the red and blue paint no longer exist, like they've been completely destroyed and replaced by an entirely new paint that wasn't there before. However, that's not true, right? No, they still exist. They're still there, just really, *really* closely combined together on the page. This is a good way to picture the Incarnation: God becoming a Galilean.*

* Galilee is the name of the region in the north of what is today the country of Israel. It's where Jesus grew up and started His ministry.

Why does His 'hypostasis' even matter? Actually, it's very important. In fact, it is closely connected with the reason God the Father sent Jesus: to save the world. More precisely, He sent Jesus to redeem—that means 'set free' or 'liberate'—us from what I (Father Ben) sometimes simply call, 'The Bad': our brokenness; our 'fallenness', our frustrating…finitude. This unhappy condition**—our total *depravity*—is like itchy, uncomfortable underwear we can't ever take off! *Urgh.* —not by ourselves; not without *super*-natural help.

To save us, then, He had to remove the problem, the obstacle: *sin*. That's the badness, the fallenness, I just mentioned. However, there's so much! Have you seen it? It's *everywhere*: in the newspapers, on TV, in the mirror even! (I'm talking about you and me.) There's war and bullying and, well, you know... Who could fix all that? The sin of every person—*all* seven to eight billion of us? It would take a superhero to do that, right? Exactly! An *ordinary* man couldn't. An *ordinary* man's death wouldn't be *commensurate*. (Ooh, great word! But do you know what it means? Ask your course-leader, grab a dictionary, or look online. It may help to think of a set of old-fashioned kitchen scales.)

** The word "condition" is one we will see Cranmer uses in Article X. We're going to discuss this topic in more detail when we come to look at Articles IX, X, and XI. However—spoiler alert—I'll put it here in brief: God became a man to change us completely into something more like Him. What was He? Do you remember? Turn back to Article I and look at numbers 1 through 3.

Article III
Of the Going down of Christ into Hell

Having wowed many people by what He said and what He did, Jesus died—*painfully*. He was abandoned by most of His friends. He was crucified (on a cross) by enemies who envied and feared His popularity. However, that wasn't the end. Luke writes,

> A man named Joseph was a member of the Jewish Council [of priests]. He was a good and honest man. Joseph had not agreed with what the leaders had decided and done. He was from Arimathea, a town in Judea. He himself was waiting for God's kingdom. Joseph went to Pilate and asked for Jesus's body. Joseph took it down and wrapped it in linen cloth. Then he placed it in a tomb cut in the rock. (Lk 23:50–53a)

What do you think happened next? It's exciting, but don't shout out! Write your answer below.

Answer:

_____

_____

_____

Yes, He did—and that's incredible; *the* most incredible thing to have happened *ever*—since the 'Big Bang', at least. (That's what we call the beginning of the universe.) However, you have, in fact—not surprisingly, mind—missed a step. There was an important event that took place *between* Jesus's death on Friday and the Resurrection on Sunday. I'll let Cranmer tell you—it's what Article III is all about:

As Christ died for us, and was buried, so also is it to be believed, that He went down into Hell.

I said I wasn't surprised that you overlooked this fact because the four gospels—those are the biographies about Jesus written by Matthew, Mark, Luke and John—do not *explicitly* mention this happening. *But wait!* Peter, the fisherman, one of Jesus's closest friends (like His BFF, in fact) wrote about it in *his* letters, which you can find near the end of the New Testament.

In those letters he tells us that Jesus, even as His body lay dead, visited a mysterious place to visit with "the spirits in Prison" (1 Pet 3:19). This "Prison" was Sheol, where the Old Testament tells us that all the souls of everyone from long, long ago were waiting: the prophet Job, for example, warned, "The least important and most important people are there," even "princes who used to have gold" (3:19 and 14). It is often described, especially in the

Psalms, as a huge, dark hole. Some people used to think that if we just dug deep enough, we'd find it! We won't; as the theologian Oliver O'Donovan explains, "[Sheol] has no point of intersection with our time-space universe."[4]

Why is Article III important? It concerns the character of God. As we've learned, Jesus said that "'No one comes to the Father except through me'" (Jn 14:6). By that, He meant, "No one can enjoy God's (holy) company in the New Jerusalem"—what we normally call Heaven—"without my help." Yet, there were hundreds of thousands—*millions*—of men, women, boys, and girls who died in ancient times before Jesus came into the world to tell them that they needed His help. Jesus never told the cavemen, for example, in the Stone Age. Is it fair that they lived too soon to be saved?

After all, imagine I had a bag of delicious candies—the old-fashioned ones that taste like rhubarb and custard (*yum!*)—and I divided them evenly between my friends five minutes before you arrived, although I knew you were on your way. How would you feel if you missed out on having one for yourself just because of timing, which you couldn't help? You would think the person who gave the candies to everyone but you wasn't very nice, right? God, however, the prophet Isaiah tells us, "is a God who is *always* fair. Blessed are all those who wait for Him to act." (Is 30:18) Accordingly, God sent Jesus not just to Earth to share the 'Good News' *with the living*, that they could have life after death by the gift** of His crucifixion; He sent Him even further than that: to Sheol too; to preach in 'the Land of the Dead' itself! (Cranmer says "Hell" in the Article, but that word is a bit misleading these days.*) And when some of the souls languishing there heard what Jesus had to say, with joy, we're told, they "came out of the[ir] tombs... [and] went into the Holy City[, Jerusalem, where] they appeared to many people" (Mt 27:53). *Boo!*

Now, what, exactly, did it look like when Jesus went to Sheol, a visit sometimes called, 'The Harrowing'? We don't know: the Bible is a bit light on the details. But many artists—Roman Catholic ones especially, have used their imaginations to recreate the scene. One painting I (Father Ben) like in particular is by Fra Angelico. 'Google' it now or ask your course-leader to project the painting onto a wall, perhaps; or to show you on his or her smartphone. Go on! Take a look...

Do you see the old man at the front with the long, white beard? I wonder who that is? Abraham? Moses? Notice how Jesus has smashed the door to the ground—*wham!*—with force, presumably, but then gently stretches out His hand to invite those ancient souls to escape with Him. I bet they were very pleased. Phew!

* Why do I (Father Ben) think it is misleading that Cranmer says Jesus went to "Hell"? Well, nowadays when we speak of Hell we usually mean that place the Bible says the wicked will be sent for punishment following their judgment on the Final Day. In other words, if you hear a *modern* person talking about Hell, he or she is almost certainly referring to "the lake of fire that burns with sulphur" mentioned in (the Book of) *Revelation* (21:8), which is definitely *not* the place Cranmer was talking about in the 1500s. However, languages evolve; they change.

**How is Jesus's crucifixion a "gift" with power to do such a thing? We're going to talk about that in our discussion about some of the later Articles, I promise.

---

[4] Oliver O'Donovan, *On the Thirty-Nine Articles: A Conversation with Tudor Christianity* (London: SCM Press, 2011), 33.

Article IV
Of the Resurrection of Christ

Christ did truly rise again from death, and took again His body, with flesh, bones, and all things appertaining to the perfection of man's nature; wherewith He ascended into Heaven, and there sitteth, until He return to judge all men at the last day.

Jesus's death is the focus, *the heart*, of Christianity. (That's why we see the Cross everywhere: in jewellery, on buildings, and so on.) Does it matter, then, that He came alive again afterwards? *Yes.* There are a number of reasons—three, at least.

1. It proved, once and for all, that He is exactly who He said He was: *more* than human. His death, therefore, must have much *more* meaning than the death of an ordinary person, as we will come to learn later (in this course).

2. It proved that the stuff we're made of (matter) *matters.* What we do with it, therefore, *is* a holy person's concern. I should, then, avoid doing needless damage to my body, for example, or to the body of someone *or something* else.

   I (Father Ben) think, for example, that you can tell a lot about a person by watching how he or she treats a tree when that person thinks he or she is alone. Do you find yourself thoughtlessly tearing off leaves and snapping branches during a walk in the woods or when you're playing in the yard? Maybe you enjoy the sound of that "crack"? It is true God gave trees for our enjoyment and use: in the first book of the Bible, *Genesis*, He says, "Let them [human beings] rule over all the creatures" (1:26). However, that doesn't mean we should vandalize them! After all, a good ruler, you will agree, I think, is a ruler who is *tender* toward those in his or her care, and understands that they actually need each other—that they have a *reciprocal* relationship. (*Ooh*, another great word! Maybe it's time to buy a dictionary?)

Finally,

3. There have been some "Christians" who didn't think that Jesus rose from His tomb. They taught that He came back, yes, but as a ghost(!) because He didn't want His body anymore. These people were the Docetists, and they were wrong. Saint Ignatius of Antioch (who was eaten by lions), for example, criticised the Docetists for failing to appreciate the overwhelming evidence that Jesus was, as Cranmer says, "flesh [and] bones" both before *and after* the Resurrection. Indeed, He proved as much by eating breakfast with the Apostles on the beach before rising in the sky to return to His throne with the Father (see Lk 24:42). After all, to eat any kind of meal

you need teeth, right? You need a tongue too, and a throat, guts, and things like that—a body! This reveals something very exciting indeed:

Anyone who comes back from the dead in Jesus's name (with His help) can also expect to be "flesh [and] bones" like Him. This is the hope of the Church: not to float around one day among clouds up there somewhere, playing a harp—like you see Itchy and Scratchy often do in *The Simpsons*. We are to enjoy our bodies in eternity—yes, that body you're using at this very moment to read these words. These bodies, we are told, will be made even better and stronger; they will be made "*glorious*" (see 1 Cor 15:35–49) by the power of God, and we will enjoy them right here on an improved, mended "new earth" (Rev 21:1).

Article V
Of the Holy Ghost

We've so far discussed only two out of the *three* persons that, together, combine to form the *one* (true) God Christians worship. Now we come to the last of them: the Holy Ghost, also called—these days, 'the Holy Spirit'. Sadly—*scandalously*—He's overlooked or neglected by some Christians. Cranmer himself, in fact, forgot to mention Him when the Articles were first written: *Oops!* Another Archbishop of Canterbury, therefore, Matthew Parker, inserted this text in 1563:

The Holy Ghost, proceeding from the Father and the Son, is of one substance, majesty, and glory, with the Father and the Son, very and eternal God.

He is called by a number of different names in the Holy Scriptures, such as "Sophia," which means 'wisdom', and "the Paraclete." (Paraclete is an old Greek word for a lawyer or advocate.) This is a professional arguer who stands with an accused person in a courtroom, and tries to help that person by, for example, pointing out any mistakes in the claims being made against him or her.

Maybe those mistakes are obvious, such as the police having arrested the wrong person; they were looking for someone called "Will," but your name is "Bill." Furthermore, the courtroom can be a loud and scary place, and the people who work there use strange, long words that you don't understand (jargon). Maybe you're shy and become tongue-tied speaking in front of crowds? These are all reasons why a person uses an "advocate."

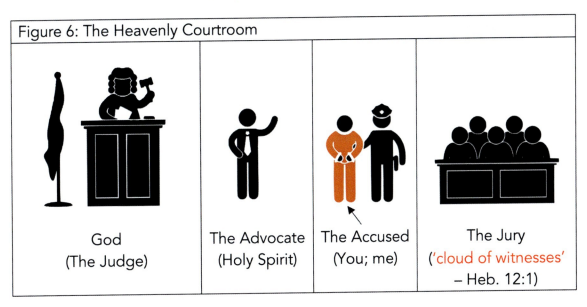

Figure 6: The Heavenly Courtroom

| God (The Judge) | The Advocate (Holy Spirit) | The Accused (You; me) | The Jury ('cloud of witnesses' – Heb. 12:1) |

For example, let's say you worked as the janitor in a school. And you mopped a floor with soapy water and a visitor slipped and fell, hurting herself. That person—the one who had the accident, embarrassed and upset, might accuse you of *deliberately* trying to hurt her. Well, an advocate would speak on your behalf to the judge, pointing out that you only did the job you were paid to do: keeping things clean. A wet, soapy floor might be dangerous, yes—because it is slippery, but that doesn't mean you hoped or *intended* to endanger anybody. To prove this, your accuser would have to offer the court something called 'evidence', like a diary entry where you described a criminal motive.

In other words, a 'paraclete' (an advocate) is somebody whose purpose—the main thing that he or she does—is to help those who can't help themselves. That means *us*. This is exactly what we find being said about the Holy Spirit in the New Testament. God "will give [Him]" to those trying to "obey my commands [the Law]... He lives with you, and He will be in you" (Jn 14:15–17), in order that "our lives can be useful to God" (Rm 7:4b). Yes, the prophet Micah puts it this way: "The Spirit of the LORD has filled me with power. He helps me do what is fair; He makes me brave" (3:8).

That power is the very same power by which God created the universe and by which Jesus made blind people see, paralyzed men walk, etc. If He—the Spirit, that is—is inside of us, we *too* can expect to perform miracles. (See: John 14:12.) These miracles may not include walking on water and so on, but, certainly, if nothing else, they could include miracles of personal transformation: significant changes in our characters; miracles of becoming more...*holy*. (We're going to talk about this process when we discuss Articles X and XII.)

I say: let's invite the Spirit into our lives now—with a song, perhaps? How about "Come Thou Fount of Every Blessing"? This has been a very popular hymn since the mid-eighteenth century. It uses poetry to describe the Spirit as a spring of refreshing water, provided by the kindness of God for sinners, like you and me, as we journey through the world and battle with The Bad and its temptations.

(Your course-leader could play the music from a smartphone or use a CD.)

Come, thou Fount of every blessing,
tune my heart to sing thy grace;
streams of mercy, never ceasing,
call for songs of loudest praise.
Teach me some melodious sonnet,
sung by flaming tongues above.
Praise the mount I'm fixed upon it
mount of God's redeeming love.

Here I find my greatest treasure;
hither by thy help I've come;
and I hope, by thy good pleasure,
safely to arrive at home.

Jesus sought me when a stranger,
wandering from the fold of God;
He, to rescue me from danger,
bought me with His precious blood.

Oh, to grace how great a debtor
daily I'm constrained to be!
Let thy goodness, like a fetter,
bind my wandering heart to thee:
prone to wander, LORD, I feel it,
prone to leave the God I love;
here's my heart, O take and seal it;
seal it for thy courts above.

SESSION 5

Article VI
Of the Sufficiency of the Holy Scriptures for Salvation

Holy Scripture containeth all things necessary to salvation: so that whatsoever is not read therein, nor may be proved thereby, is not to be required of any man, that it should be believed as an Article of the Faith, or be thought requisite or necessary to salvation. In the name of the Holy Scripture we do understand those canonical books of the Old and New Testament, of whose authority was never any doubt in the Church.

I said before (in the Introduction: Part 1) that the Bible, or Holy Scriptures, are the Word of the LORD, "breathed" from the "mouth" (that is, *the mind*) of God (see 2 Tim 3:16). We also said that He used several different people to write it. In what way is this true, exactly? Well, one person describes the miracle of divine inspiration in this way:

> When you use a pen to write a letter or a note, the pen puts the ink on the page and the ink forms the words. When the letter is complete, you could say the pen was the instrument for writing the letter. Yet if your hand did not move the pen, it could write nothing. In a similar way, the writers of the Bible—with their own personalities and language—were like pens in the hand of God. God inspired them to remember what they saw and to write down what God wanted them to write. So while the Bible was written by people, God was the author behind it.[5]

This makes the Bible a unique book and extremely precious. (Do you remember what I told you the Archbishop of Canterbury said about the Bible when it was handed to King Charles?) Notice what Cranmer says: it "containeth" (has inside of it) not *everything* we may want to learn; it can't, for example, tell us how to fix a car or harpoon a fish. It doesn't seem to care all that much about atoms or astronomy either. You won't find in it delicious recipes for dinner tonight. Ultimately, however, this information isn't as important as what we *do* find in the Bible.

For this reason, during his lifetime (that period we call, 'The Reformation'), many Christians, like Cranmer, were attempting to mend and heal the Church of some serious mistakes that had crept into its practice and theology. And a lot of the new, Reformed congregations (those few that accepted change was necessary) chose to make a new start by putting the Bible at the heart of their worship in place of sharing the Eucharist (Communion). More precisely, that is to say, some congregations put *preaching* (the giving of the sermon) at the heart. You can see this development very clearly when you look at how they chose to arrange the interiors of their chapels. Ask your

---

[5] Marty Machowski, *The Ology: Ancient Truths Ever New* (Greensboro, NC: New Growth Press, 2015), 225.

course-leader (the person teaching today) to find an image of the interior of the Old South Meeting House in Boston, for example. From your experience as an Anglican, what's missing? Let me rephrase the question: What would *you* expect to see as the "liturgical center"[6] in a church, and then look for that thing in the photos. Write your answer in the box below.

Answer:

_____

_____

_____

Yes! I've even seen the Communion table on wheels, so that it can be rolled out when it's needed (which is not very often) and then rolled away again.

Oliver O'Donovan observes that Anglican Christians (like the 'Episcopalians' in America) did something else entirely: they opted for a *third* way. Yes, since the time of Cranmer, we Anglicans put "the ordered *reading* of Holy Scripture, rather than the exposition of it [i.e., the sermon, at] the centre [of our worship]."[7] That's why we always have at least three but sometimes *four(!)* passages from the Bible on a Sunday, like an epistle *and* a psalm *and* something from one of the gospels, and so on. After all, what's better than a single scoop of ice cream? *Two scoops!* Or as much as you can get.

---

[6] James White, *Protestant Worship and Church Architecture* (Eugene, OR: Wipf & Stock, 2003), 34.
[7] O'Donovan, 46. (My emphasis.)

Article VII
Of the Old Testament

The Old Testament is not contrary to the New: for both in the Old and New Testament everlasting life is offered to mankind by Christ, who is the only mediator between God and man, being both God and man. Wherefore they are not to be heard, which feign that the old Fathers did look only for transitory promises. Although the Law given from God by Moses, as touching ceremonies and rites, do not bind Christian men, nor the civil precepts thereof ought of necessity to be received in any commonwealth; yet notwithstanding, no Christian man whatsoever is free from the obedience of the Commandments which are called moral.

The Bible, which is—in reality, to be precise—a *library* of sacred books, has two halves. I say "halves" but, truthfully, the first 'half'—that is to say, the *Old* Testament—is much, much longer than the second. And although these 'testaments' can seem rather different in a number of ways, when we look closer, in fact, the message is the same: There is one God; He loves His people, and so hates their sin ('The Bad'); and He is determined to fix the problem. You can see this message on nearly every page, from *Genesis* (the first book of the Bible) to *Revelation* (the last). After all, this is just what you should expect to find when you consider the character of God as He has revealed Himself: consider — "Jesus Christ is the same yesterday and today and forever" (Heb 13:8). And: "God...doesn't change His mind...He makes a promise, and then He keeps it" (See Num 23:19).

It is for this reason, you see, that Cranmer adds here, in Article VII, why Christians cannot just ignore the Commandments given to Moses thousands of years ago: because they remain a good guide—the *best guide*(!)—as to what sort of behavior pleases God, like honesty and kindness to strangers.

Article VIII
Of the Three Creeds

The Three Creeds, Nicene Creed, Athanasius' Creed, and that which is commonly called the Apostles' Creed, ought thoroughly to be received and believed: for they may be proved by most certain warrants of holy Scripture.

Because the Bible is a library of many books—*sixty-six*, in fact—the Church has invented tools to help us summarize (that is, "to make small") their contents. These are "the Creeds." They are lists of theological true statements. Many Christians use one of these lists or *creeds* every week during their Sunday worship. Usually, it's the Nicene Creed. Cranmer, though, reminds us of two other helpful creeds: the Athanasian and the Apostles' Creed. His enthusiasm for them emphasizes how Anglicanism *wasn't* a new religion—*oh not at all*—but, actually, a return to the historic (Christian) faith as taught by the twelve disciples to their friends.

These Creeds were written in either Latin (the language of the Romans) or in Greek by the leaders of the Church called, "bishops." They would gather, in their hundreds, at the summer palace of Caesar Constantine (or somewhere else fancy) to give their approval to the Creeds by shouting, *"Néi!"* ("Yes"). This was necessary because there was at that time a growing confusion caused by certain men, whose theology was, well...less than great.

Less-than-great theology, or mistaken theology (that is, theology that doesn't reflect the God-breathed Bible) is called *heresy*. Today, there are still people who spread wrong thinking and share false statements about God. Jesus warned us about such people: "Watch out for *false* prophets," He said. "They come to you pretending to be sheep. But on the inside they are hungry wolves" (Mt 7:15). Indeed, it can be very confusing deciding who to trust.

Some heresies, however, are easy to recognize because they take their theology not just from the Bible. They mix in other writings too, which only pretend to be God-breathed. Knowing which books are truly inspired by Him, therefore, is the best way to protect ourselves. Do you know them all? What about those in the Old Testament?

Fill in the blanks completing the words below.

1. G ___ n e _____ s

2. ___ x o _____

3. L e ___ i t i c _____

4. N _____ e ___ s

5. D e u t _____ n o ___ y

6. J ___ s h ___ a

7. J ___ d g e ___

8. R _____ h

9. 1 ___ a ___ u e l

10. ___ S _____

11. 1 K _____

12. 2 _____ g s

13. ___ C h r _____

14. 2 C _____

15. E z ___ a

16. N ___ h ___ m _____ h

17. E s t h _____

18. ___ o b

19. P s _____ s

20. P ___ o _____ b ___

21. E c c l e s _____ s _____ s

22. S _____ g o f S _____ s

23. I s _____ a h

24. ___ e r e m _____ h

25. L ___ m ___ n t ___ t _____ n s

26. E z e _____ l

27. ___ a n i e l

28. H o ___ e a

29. ___ o e l

30. A _____ s

31. O b a d ___ a h

32. J _____ h
33. M i c ___
34. N a ____ m
35. H ___ b ___ k k ___ k
36. ___ e p h a n i a h
37. ___ a ___ g a i
38. Z ___ c h a r i a h
39. ___ a l a c h i

SESSION 6

Article IX
Of Original or Birth-Sin

Original Sin standeth not in the following of Adam, (as the Pelagians[*] do vainly talk), but it is the fault and corruption of the nature of every man, that naturally is ingendered of the offspring of Adam; whereby man is very far gone from original righteousness, and is of his own nature inclined to evil, so that the flesh lusteth always contrary to the spirit; and therefore in every person born into this world, it deserveth God's wrath and damnation. And this infection of nature doth remain, yea in them that are regenerated; whereby the lust of the flesh, called in the Greek, 'Phronema Sarkos', which some do expound the wisdom, some sensuality, some the affection, some the desire, of the flesh, is not subject to the Law of God. And although there is no condemnation for them that believe and are baptized, yet the Apostle doth confess, that concupiscence and lust hath of itself the nature of sin.

> * Pelagians? Who are they? They were followers of a British heretic called, "Pelagius." He lived in Britain in the fourth and fifth centuries AD, and we're told by his opponents that he taught that people are basically good even without the Spirit of God; they just need to be reasoned with. This is a very naïve—and *incorrect*—worldview.

What is sin? Well, quoting the Bible, we've already said that God hates it, and we know He is good. Sin, then, must be the opposite of what He wants. Where, then, does it come from, since He created everything? (See Article I.) Well, there is that famous story, of course, in the Book of *Genesis* in which Adam and Eve, an ancient couple, ate fruit from a tree that God had forbidden them to touch. Do you know it? It's very famous. Was sin hiding in that fruit, like a virus that infected (made sick) humanity? *No.* Remember, creation (the world) was, in the beginning, "very good" (Gen 1:31). God said so again and again. We must be careful, therefore, to interpret that significant, early moment with Adam and Eve accurately. What Cranmer observes is that sin came from *within* Adam and his wife; sin was their *choice* to disobey God.

This mistake (Adam choosing to ignore God and decide for himself how to behave) corrupted who he was. It was like dropping a tiny amount of blue or black ink into a large glass of clear water: eventually, the ink colors all of the liquid and makes it ugly and undrinkable. In other words, sin *changed* Adam, and this same, unhappy change "came" to the rest of us too (Rom 5:12).

How did this happen?! As Saint Augustine of Hippo explains, "We were all in that one man…[though w]e did not yet possess forms individually created and assigned to us."[8] In other words, "We were all in [him]" (like the smaller, nesting dolls inside of a Russian Matryoshka doll) because he was an ancestor of us all—we descend from him (see *Acts* 17:26). That is to say—to use modern words: we have his DNA, his genetics. It is, therefore, as Cranmer observes, our "nature." Let me put this even more simply. Just like a banana is yellow, elephants have trunks, and mice squeak, we sin because we are sinners. It is who we are.

---

8 Qtd. in Jesse Couenhoven, "St. Augustine's Doctrine of Original Sin," *Augustinian Studies* 36, No. 2 (2005): 367.

Article X
Of Free Will

The condition of man after the fall of Adam is such, that he cannot turn and prepare himself, by his own natural strength and good works, to faith, and calling upon God: Wherefore we have no power to do good works pleasant and acceptable to God, without the grace of God by Christ preventing us, that we may have a good will, and working with us, when we have that good will.

During this course we've been reminded of how our nature—what we *are*—is corrupted: we've used terms like 'depraved' and 'fallen' to describe this 'condition'. Now, in Article X, Cranmer explains how, because of this corruption, we "cannot turn" to God and respond to His goodness as we ought to; that is, with the correct amount of urgency and thankfulness. And the problem is our *will*. The 'will' is, for lack of a better word, a person's 'choosing-engine': Shall I do 'this' or shall I do 'that'? It's in our brains, our minds. A corrupted 'will' doesn't even know something is wrong! It just makes bad choices repeatedly, like a scratched Blu-ray that keeps skipping in the player, so that the actors in a movie say the same line over and over again, stuck on repeat. Very, very annoying!

The corrupted will can't even appropriately respond to the wonderful Gospel and believe that some will enjoy an eternal life with Jesus after the General Resurrection if only they put their faith in Him. This is like a person who's told that if he or she just saves his or her pocket money (allowance) and does not spend it, one day he or she could buy something really great, like an iPad or a car. Instead, the person spends it immediately on lots of little temporary things such as bubble gum, which grows hard, loses its flavor, and has to be thrown away—*urgh!* Gross.

Have you ever disappointed yourself this way? I know I have. Well, just as a broken engine inside of a car can't mend itself—it needs a mechanic, we *too* need someone to fix *our* wills, our minds. *That* "mechanic" is the Holy Spirit. We began talking about Him in Article V. "To everyone" He has been given, says Saint John, as a "light" (Jn 1:9), "preventing" (Cranmer's word) each person from *only* making bad choices all the time, and enabling each person to make some good ones too.

This theology of a "preventing," or *prevenient*, grace was significantly expanded by an Anglican priest in the seventeenth-century named John Wesley. He argued that the Spirit was everywhere in the world, preparing every man and woman, boy and girl, to hear people like him preach the Good News that they have a loving Father in Heaven who wants to save them from their corruption and the bad that they do.

To prove this, Wesley took a ship to Georgia (in America) across the wide, dangerous Atlantic Ocean, from his home in England. He hiked deep into the forest to tell the Yamacraw Indians who lived there about Jesus. It was a very brave thing to do! He preached to the African slaves in the towns as well. Both of these groups were being ignored by the Church, which was *very* shameful. However, Wesley knew better. He knew that the grace (*the love*) of God extended to include them too.

Article XI
Of the Justification of Humankind

Earlier, I promised to tell you how it is that by Jesus's death on the Cross you and I can live with God in a wonderful place called the "New Jerusalem" (in the "new earth"). Today, finally, this is our subject: So, how *does* a person qualify to go there? Well, frankly, *he* or *she* doesn't. Because a person, we learn in the Bible, must be "righteous." That means 'perfect'! —always thinking and choosing what *God* would think and choose. Otherwise, an ordinary person would spoil *that* amazing place—the New Jerusalem—with their sin ('The Bad'), just like we're spoiling this lovely world we already live in. Yes, we're not righteous, are we? (Be honest!) We're not righteous because, as we've learned, we're 'corrupted'—that's the word we used in our discussion of Article II and, just now, about Article X. This is why we find Cranmer saying in Article XI the following:

We are accounted righteous before God only for the merit of our Lord and Saviour Jesus Christ by faith, and not for our own works or deservings: wherefore, that we are justified by faith only is a most wholesome doctrine, and very full of comfort, as more largely is expressed in "The Homily of Justification."

In other words, Jesus faced *all* the same temptations we do, but He never gave in to 'The Bad'—to sin. He conquered the human condition! He made our nature *nice*—truly. (See 1 Pet 2:22.) Then, much to everyone's surprise, He went to die anyway to take the punishment from God that *we* deserve—Saint Paul calls it "[our] curse" (Gal 3:13). He went to die, that is, for the many, many times you and I have disappointed the LORD and displeased Him with our lies, jealousies, thefts, and violence, etc. As the prophet Isaiah explains: "the LORD has placed on His servant the sins of all of us" (Is 53:6). Why does this matter?

Well, when I (Father Ben) was growing up, there was on the wall of a classroom in my school a list of all the students. And when you did something that the teacher liked (your homework and so on), she would stick a little gold-paper star next to your name. These stars were then counted at the end of the week and, depending on how many you'd been given, you got a prize! Like chocolate, or a Hot-Wheels racer. Well, in (the Book of) *Revelation* (at the end of the New Testament), the author—John—is taken on a tour of God's heavenly palace, and he sees there "the Book of Life" in which our whole lives are recorded—everything we have ever done and said and thought. Specifically, 'The Bad'—the *bad* stuff we've done (to others): (see Rev 20:12). The Book of Life, then, is like the list I just described, but in opposite-world. That is to say: the long record of our sin will act *against* us like a dirty, black stain at the time of Judgment, which is called "the Day of the LORD." However, Jesus took this 'stain', we've learned, and made it His own: "He bec[a]me sin," explains Paul, the Apostle (2 Cor 5:21). And in its place Jesus offers— or "imputes"—to us His holiness, His go(o)dness, His sticky 'gold-paper stars' that He earned for *actually* keeping the Law. And for this swap; this *exchange* to take place, which is called (by theologians) 'justification', all you need to do is, *sincerely*, "Say with your mouth, 'Jesus is Lord.' [And b]elieve in your heart that God raised Him from the dead" (Rom 10:9). *This* is what it means when someone says to you, "Have faith." He or she simply means, 'trust that these tremendous truths—the truths of the Gospel—apply *to you*'.

SESSION 7

Article XII
Of Good Works

You might say that faith in Christ—trusting Him—is the key that opens the 'lock' to life-after-death with God in the New Jerusalem in the new earth; and Jesus's death is the door—*the way in*. You know, *He* actually said about His own death (on the Cross) that it was "the price" of our admission to the Kingdom. *Ouch!* (See Mt 20:28 and Mk 10:45)

Does that make sense? Let me put it another way… When I was a young man (a foolish one!), I would go nightclubbing on Fridays with my best-friend, 'Tris'. Now at first, I wasn't old enough to be admitted; I was 'under-age', but the doormen who were supposed to keep out minors like me *loved* Tris: he was a charmer! (And he looked older than he was.) Whenever we were together, therefore, they would let us *both* enter, yes, but only for *his* sake. Trusting Christ for salvation, then, is the same as when I trusted Tris was my ticket to a good time: *he* was the one who made my fun possible, just as Jesus's sacrifice makes it possible that I—or anyone else for that matter—can be saved.

But you know what? I think I can offer an even better analogy: Confessing my need for Christ is like pressing 'Engine Start' on my Hyundai. That's a necessary step if I've decided to drive my car somewhere today. But it can't move (even if I push the button a hundred times) without the *power* unleashed from the combustion of gas (petrol) in the engine. And, similarly, it is Christ's crucifixion that makes my faith *efficacious* (fruitful; of consequence). It's. That. Simple. Or is it?! —despite Jesus's clarity on this subject, it wasn't too long before some of His followers (in the early Medieval Church) began to question if His death really was…'sufficient'. Huh?

Figure 7: What is "sufficiency"?

Insufficient

Yes, we might be tempted to ask: "Is it enough that *Jesus* died when really it is I who deserve the fate He suffered on the Cross?" This led some theologians to suggest that perhaps people like us need to add something…*extra* to earn that gift of 'justification' we were talking about in our discussion of Article XI. This 'extra' thing might be walking to the Holy Land (a pilgrimage); standing in a river in winter, naked, freezing, whilst saying prayers; or, sitting on top of a pillar for a whole year, exposed to the wind and rain; and other such unpleasant activities. —these are all things that Christians have attempted: just 'Google' Simeon Stylites, for example.

Fortunately, in the 1500s, not long before Cranmer came along, a German monk, Martin Luther, challenged this confusion. He found the answer in Saint Paul's letter to the *Romans*, which states, "Christ died for us" (Rm 5:8). And that's it! —it's more than enough.

So, I can relax now, right? *Yes...and no.* If you're a Christian, "yes," you can relax thanks to what Jesus has achieved; you can know that "[the LORD] will never leave you. He'll never desert you" (Deut 31:8). However, Cranmer added this important, not-to-be-forgotten caveat in Article XII:

> *Albeit that good works, which are the fruits of faith, and follow after justification, cannot put away our sins, and endure the severity of God's judgment; yet are they pleasing and acceptable to God in Christ, and do spring out necessarily of a true and lively faith; insomuch that by them a lively faith may be as evidently known as a tree discerned by the fruit.*

In other words, Cranmer is saying this: that *real* faith—faith I sincerely feel as genuine gratitude that Jesus took the "curse" (the punishment) for sin—*will* change my behavior. After all, we've talked about the Holy Spirit making us better, kinder people (see Article V). He also, we learned, is the very same One who helped us trust in the Good News of Jesus's crucifixion in the first place (see Article X). If He's already there inside of me, then, giving me my faith, it will eventually become obvious to others, right? Indeed, Luther observed that a *true* Christian's *whole* life becomes unending "repentance;" not just saying "thank you" to God but actually turning our gratitude into *action*—making it evident (visible to those around us) by choosing what Christ would choose and avoiding what He would avoid.

How could you act (show) your thankfulness in the world to friends, family, and strangers?

Answer:

_____

_____

_____

Article XIII
Of Works before Justification

Works done before the grace of Christ, and the Inspiration of his Spirit, are not pleasant to God, forasmuch as they spring not of faith in Jesus Christ, neither do they make men meet to receive grace, or (as the School-authors say) deserve grace of congruity: yea rather, for that they are not done as God hath willed and commanded them to be done, we doubt not but they have the nature of sin.

Luther's reminder to the Church that salvation is

angered lots of people. In fact, to keep him safe from his enemies, a friend of his, the Elector of Saxony, a rich nobleman called, "Frederick the Wise," pretended to kidnap Luther, and brought him to his castle in Wartburg, Eisenach. Here, Luther was able to continue working and writing about the Bible, and his courageous work inspired many others, including Thomas Cranmer (as we will see later, when we come to discuss Article XXVIII).

One of the theological ideas that became clear to Luther through his study of the Bible was that only through the help of the Holy Spirit can people be *consistently* good. And until the Spirit comes to live in a person, all that person does is, as the prophet Isaiah explained, "like dirty rags" (64:6).

Although this is hard to hear, it's important. Why? As I said at the very beginning of this course, "right thinking leads to right action."

That's the end of another session. *Phew!* I hope you're enjoying it. There's a lot to think about, right? Does your head hurt? Well, if you're looking for something to do with your *hands*, how about building the castle where Luther was protected while he did his important studying and writing?— The company Schreiber-Bogen has one for sale that is fantastic. You can buy it on Amazon. It's a really big model, so it'll take you some time to build, but you could get started now. Grab a glue-stick, a thin metal ruler (for making sharp folds), and some scissors. Good luck!

Article XIV
Of Works of Supererogation

Voluntary works besides, over, and above, God's commandments, which they call works of supererogation, cannot be taught without arrogancy and impiety: for by them men do declare, that they do not only render unto God as much as they are bound to do, but that they do more for his sake, than of bounden duty is required: whereas Christ saith plainly, "When ye have done all that are commanded to you, say, we are unprofitable servants."

Fearing God—as we should, for He is our judge, and "[t]he eyes of the Lord are everywhere." (Prov. 15:3) And doubting that Jesus's death was fully sufficient to fix our broken relationship with Him, I told you last time that some Christians have occasionally tried *extreme* things—things not commanded in the Bible, like giving away their wives to nunneries or living in caves. It is true that there are some pretty odd people among the heroes of Scripture: there's John the Baptist who ate locusts, and Ezekiel who cut off his own hair with a sword and burned it in a fire! Such people are called, "eccentrics." Jesus did none of these things, of course, and He is, as Saint Peter teaches, "[our] example." (See 1 Pet 2:21.) Furthermore, Moses added, "Don't turn to the right or the left" (Deut 28:14). In other words, do *exactly* as Christ taught, not less or more, and God will be pleased with you.

Furthermore, we find Cranmer criticizing extreme, eccentric behavior ("works of supererogation," as he calls it) because, very often, such behavior is reliant on, or requires, the help of so-called 'normal' Christians. For example: a man who decides to go live deep in the desert to pray, continuously, night and day (called a hermit) needs other people to *not* do that but instead to grow vegetables and produce food that he can eat. It is wrong, therefore, to say that the hermit is more holy than the men and women who provide for his needs. Indeed, you might *even* say that they are being less selfish than him! After all, *they* are the ones being charitable as the Savior said we ought.

Article XV
Of Christ Alone without Sin

Christ in the truth of our nature was made like unto us in all things, sin only except, from which He was clearly void, both in His flesh, and in His spirit. He came to be the lamb without spot, who, by sacrifice of Himself once made, should take away the sins of the world, and sin, as Saint John saith, was not in Him. But all we the rest, although baptized, and born again in Christ, yet offend in many things; and if we say we have no sin, we deceive ourselves, and the truth is not in us.

Our gratitude for Jesus's death grows when we reflect on how deserving *we* are of that punishment* and on how *un*-deserving Jesus was to be hurt in that horrid way. So, Cranmer returns to emphasize the subject in this Article, reminding us that, in the Bible, Jesus is described as a 'lamb': "'*The Lamb*...[, who] takes away the sin of the world!'"—a gentle, innocent, grass-eating *fluff*-ball. (See Jn 1:29)

However, according to the Bible, Jesus is *also* "'The Lion of the tribe of Judah...'" And we mustn't lose sight of either identity, which hold together so tightly that, in (the Book of) *Revelation*, chapter 5, they are interchangeable! They just sort of...collapse into each other: the lamb is the lion and the lion is the lamb. Thus everyone else—"all we the rest"—can't be one or the other. Including those men who established other religions. Muhammad, for example. Or Buddha, and so on. Which is why their tombs aren't empty. They're in them! They're *dead*. That's just a fact. Even their followers admit this. Only Christ *alone* (still) lives. Only Christ alone has "'life in himself.'" (Jn 5:26) Only Christ alone is the answer; only He offers us 'abundant life'—like I promised back in Session 2. And this is something that C. S. Lewis, perhaps the most famous of all Anglicans, makes very clear in his wonderful stories about the fictional, *magical* land of 'Narnia'; which, exactly like the Articles, are a tool to help us learn good theology. Yes, just think of those stories as long parables...

In one scene, then, in *The Silver Chair*—which is my (Father Ben's) favorite scene—and favorite Narnia book, in fact; one of the protagonists—*the heroine*—"Jill Pole," is very, very thirsty—indeed, *dying* of thirst; and she sees a stream of water flowing down a hillside: *Yay!* But wait: she also notices—to her horror—that the stream is being guarded by an *enormous*, (terrifying) lion! A *talking* lion, called, "Aslan." "'Oh dear!' said Jill, coming another step nearer. 'I suppose I must go and look for another stream then.' 'There is no other stream', said the Lion."[9] So, what did she do? Well, what would *you* do? Dive in? Or complain about an imagined lack of alternative 'streams'? Does it make sense to do that if the real one is more than enough? — "...[Jill] went forward to the stream, knelt down, and began scooping up water in her hand. It was the coldest, most refreshing water she had ever tasted. You didn't need to drink much of it, for it quenched your thirst at once."[10]

---

[9] C. S. Lewis, *The Silver Chair* (New York, NY: HarperTrophy: 1981), 21.
[10] Ibid.

* Maybe you're thinking, "But *I'm not a murderer!* Are my sins (that anger and disappoint God) *really* that bad?" Yes. Remember, He is very, very special; there's only one of Him in the *whole* universe! With that in mind, imagine breaking a chicken egg by dropping it on the floor. Would that be bad? No, of course not. But now imagine a living, ancient *dinosaur* egg was discovered; it's one-of-a-kind, and you broke *that*. Now, would *that* be bad? *Of course!* It would be terrible! Because it is unique, of *unequalled* preciousness. Well, God is like that dinosaur egg, but even more…*sacred.* (Remember that word? See session 1.)

SESSION 8

Article XVI
Of Sin after Baptism

Not every deadly sin willingly committed after baptism is sin against the Holy Ghost, and unpardonable. Wherefore the grant of repentance is not to be denied to such as fall into sin after baptism. After we have received the Holy Ghost, we may depart from grace given, and fall into sin, and by the grace of God we may arise again, and amend our lives. And therefore they are to be condemned, which say, they can no more sin as long as they live here, or deny the place of forgiveness to such as truly repent.

Last time we were together, we discussed how a person is "saved." It is a process, we learned, that begins with *justification* (see Article XI). Remember? Christ, who "takes away the sin of the world" (Jn 1:29) on the Cross, replaces (He swaps) the corruption of our lives (our ungodliness, our fallenness, the stain or curse of the bad things we've said and done) for His righteousness (His perfection). We discovered that to become justified requires saying "Sorry" to God and asking Him for this marvellous gift.

In His preaching, Jesus often described what it means to become justified (to become Elect) by talking about sheep.

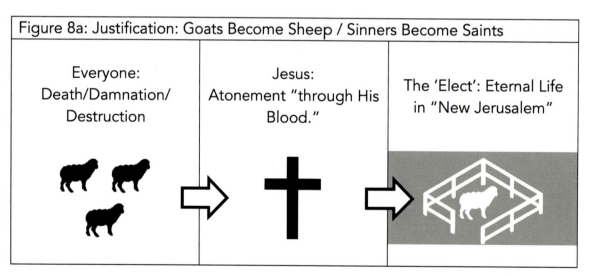

Figure 8a: Justification: Goats Become Sheep / Sinners Become Saints

Everyone: Death/Damnation/ Destruction	Jesus: Atonement "through His Blood."	The 'Elect': Eternal Life in "New Jerusalem"

However, we mustn't forget that though the Elect (the true Christians represented by the white sheep in the diagram) have Christ's righteousness, it is, as Bishop Tom Wright says, a "legal fiction"[11] because they still also have sinful natures. They're not *really* as righteous as Jesus is;

11 Tom Wright, *What Saint Paul Really Said* (Oxford: Lion, 1997), 102.

they can still make some bad choices. Because this is true, we hear Cranmer warning us that "we may depart from grace given, and fall." This isn't to frighten us, but to prepare us for the reality of following Jesus: it is often hard, and we will fail—*a lot*. What *is* dangerous, however, is if we stop being grateful and start deliberately sinning again. Then we will find ourselves in trouble at the Final Judgment. As Jesus taught, "'Not everyone who says to me, "Lord, Lord," will enter the Kingdom of Heaven. *Only* those who do what my Father in Heaven wants will enter'" (Mt 7:21).

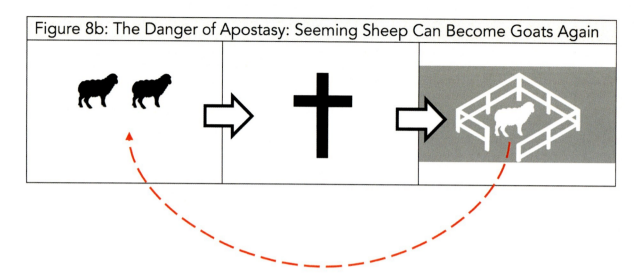

Figure 8b: The Danger of Apostasy: Seeming Sheep Can Become Goats Again

However, while we are alive and we have the Holy Spirit in us, we always have the opportunity to turn around, repent, and ask God to help us do better. He isn't, you see, eager for us to make mistakes. Oh no! Rather, what the LORD is looking for, all the time and excitedly, is *any* attempt we make to be obedient. This is like the father of the naughty prodigal son in the famous parable: "While the son was still a long way off, his father saw him [and h]e was filled with tender love for his son. He ran to him. He threw his arms around him and kissed him" (Lk 15:20). This is a window into what kind of God Christians worship. In fact, the prophet Zephaniah says that when we do choose to do what God has commanded, God is so happy that "He will sing for joy" (Zeph 3:17). What do you make of that? Wonderful, right?

Well, what's next? Cranmer's criticism of "works of supererogation" (extreme, eccentric attempts at holiness that don't resemble Jesus's own choices) was borrowed from Luther and shared by the other Reformers, and their critique was seen by the Roman Catholic Church as an attack against the monastic orders (that's the nuns and monks, some of whom had become very wealthy in reality while, supposedly, being poor in theory). It was, therefore, another cause for tension in Europe and, eventually, *war!* Yes, there was war between different kinds of Christians. And lots of people died! —it was called, "The Thirty Years War." But didn't Jesus say, "'Turn [the] other cheek'"? (See Mt 5:39.) Well, we're going to look at the issue of soldiering and fighting when we come to Article XXXVII.

Article XVII
Of Predestination and Election

Predestination to life is the everlasting purpose of God, whereby (before the foundations of the world were laid) He hath constantly decreed by His counsel secret to us, to deliver from curse and damnation those whom He hath chosen in Christ out of mankind, and to bring them by Christ to everlasting salvation, as vessels made to honour. Wherefore, they which be endued with so excellent a benefit of God be called according to God's purpose by His Spirit working in due season: they through Grace obey the calling: they be justified freely: they be made sons of God by adoption: they be made like the image of His only-begotten son, Jesus Christ: they walk religiously in good works, and at length, by God's mercy, they attain to everlasting felicity.

As the godly consideration of predestination, and our election in Christ, is full of sweet, pleasant, and unspeakable comfort to godly persons, and such as feel in themselves the working of the Spirit of Christ, mortifying the works of the flesh, and their earthly members, and drawing up their mind to high and heavenly things, as well because it doth greatly establish and confirm their faith of eternal salvation to be enjoyed through Christ, as because it doth fervently kindle their love towards God: So, for curious and carnal persons, lacking the Spirit of Christ, to have continually before their eyes the sentence of God's predestination, is a most dangerous downfall, whereby the Devil doth thrust them either into desperation, or into wretchlessness of most unclean living, no less perilous than desperation.

Furthermore, we must receive God's promises in such wise, as they be generally set forth to us in Holy Scripture: and, in our doings, that will of God is to be followed, which we have expressly declared unto us in the Word of God.

I (Father Ben) want warm Krispy-Kreme donuts like, basically, *all* the time! Oh, and hot, eggy crêpes drenched in maple syrup: *yum!* I want my wife's affection—her kisses; and, to see her smile. I want sunshine and birdsong, and for my daughter to grow up healthy and happy *and holy*; and, most importantly, I want, one day—on the *Last* Day, to hear my maker—the LORD— tell me: '"Well done, good and trustworthy [servant]; …enter into the joy of your master.'" (Mt 25:23) (To live with Him forever!) But what does *He* want? Have you ever asked yourself that question? It's a fascinating, funny one, isn't it? After all, He doesn't get hungry or bored or lonely or tired… So, obviously, He doesn't *need* anything. But what does He *want*? Well, He told us. That is to say, He told *Habakkuk*—the prophet: For "the Earth [to] be filled with the knowledge of my glory [as the waters cover the sea]." (2:14) *That's* God's 'end game'; *that's* His 'telos', (which means, 'the goal'), for creation.

Logically, then, the world we see must be *designed* to guarantee that God will get what He wants. After all, as one famous enthusiast of Article XVII explains, the seventeenth-century philosopher, Gottfried Leibniz: "[S]ince there is an infinity of possible universes in the ideas of God"—such as one where the grass is pink, for example, or another where dinosaurs never went extinct(!)—"there must be a sufficient reason for God's choice which determines Him to [make this] one rather than another."[12] That reason, Leibniz goes on to say, is its "fitness" to accomplish His pleasure; His *plan*, "which His wisdom causes God to know, His goodness makes Him choose, and His power makes Him produce."[13]

That makes sense, right? And we see evidence of this *everywhere*. Creation—the universe—isn't just a chaotic, endlessly malfunctioning, simple…*sludge*. Instead, reality resembles something more like an amazing clock or a…supercomputer! There seems to be purposeful complexity directly *and deeply* engineered into the system—visible in our bodies, in a cell, in DNA, in the stars… (This, by the way, is what's called the 'Teleological Proof for the Existence of God'.)

Now, that being said, what John the Apostle explained in one of his letters was that "knowledge" of God really means '*love of God*': see 1 Jn 4:7 (my emphasis). So, with this in mind, we can, I think, say that what God really wants is for *love* to 'fill' the Earth; that "love will grow more and more." (Phil 1:9) In other words, what God wants is the *maximal* amount of love *possible*. But, uh oh(!), love can't be faked: you can't force someone to love you; love must be *freely* felt—by 'agents'; *people* capable of making (genuine) *choices*. And that's why we're here! —Adam and Eve, and you and me, and everyone else too. But if this world is, as Leibniz would say, "*the best* of all possible worlds" from God's perspective; to achieve the *why* for which He made it, then it *must* be the one in which He *fore*-knew there *would* be people who *do* love Him: Rom 8:28-29.[14]

If God didn't use His 'foreknowledge', you see, He would risk failing to fulfil His own plan! A perfect being wouldn't—*couldn't*—do that: 'fail', that is. To fail God would have to contradict who He is, which is impossible: light can't be dark and red can't be blue. And if God 'failed' He would be less than worthy of *worship*. But to *be* God *is* to be the one who *alone* is rightfully worshipped: it's like Jesus said: "'Suppose one of you wants to build a tower. Won't you sit down first and figure out how much it will cost? Then you will see whether you have enough money to finish it. … Or suppose a king is about to go to war against another king. And suppose he has 10,000 men, while the other has 20,000 coming against him. Won't he first sit down and think about whether he can win?" (Lk 14:28-31) *Of course* he would! Well, God *is* that "king."

In other words, God gets His way; He can't be thwarted.* (Isn't that a great word!) This is the story hiding in plain sight for the person who looks for it 'beneath' the story of "Hosea" in the Old Testament: Hosea's wife was…unfaithful. She had sex with other men: uh oh! But nothing could

---

[12]   Gottfried Wilhelm Leibniz, *Philosophical Papers and Letters: Volume II*, trans. Leroy E. Loemker (Chicago, IL: The University of Chicago Press, 1956), 1053.

[13]   Ibid.

[14]   See: Irena Backus, *Leibniz: Protestant Theologian* (Oxford; New York, NY: Oxford University Press, 2016), 76-77.

prevent him—Hosea—from keeping *his* 'covenant'. Nothing—including her betrayal—was going to dissuade *him* from being who *he* had decided to be: her husband 'for better [or] for worse…till death us do part'. And God, we see in the Bible, is frequently compared to being *our* husband; the 'husband' of the Church, which is His 'bride'. (See e.g. Is 54:5) And He is determined to have *His* great 'marriage-feast'—an eternity of love in 'new heavens and the new earth'—with His saints; the 'Elect'—the *true* Christians.

Yes, as the Puritan preacher Jonathan Edwards liked to say, for them the life-to-come will be "*a world* of love:"[15] Love will 'flow' out from the LORD "in innumerable streams toward all the created inhabitants…"[16] "…there shall be no remaining enmity, or distaste, or coldness, or deadness of heart…;"[17] "not a solitary inhabitant that is not beloved by all the others."[18] And: "No inhabitants of that blessed world will ever be grieved with the thought…that their love is not *fully* and fondly returned."[19]

If you, then, having heard the Gospel (the 'Good News') find that you desire to become one of those people; *His* people, you're the reason that anything exists: He made this universe, *millions* of years ago, with *you* (in particular) in mind. (See Eph 1:4) And *this* is the meaning of 'Predestination'; that the love of God's people for Him—*your* love (if that's how you feel)—is an inevitable *re*-action to who He is. It was 'baked into the (wedding) cake' from the beginning.

---

* Did you ever get that dictionary?

---

[15] Jonathan Edwards, *Heaven Is a World of Love* (Wheaton, IL: Crossway, 2020), 35, 39, 87, 88, 90, 94, 95, 96, 103, 107, 109, 110, 111, 113.
[16] Ibid., 47
[17] 51.
[18] 49.
[19] 57.

Article XVIII
Of Obtaining Eternal Salvation Only by the Name of Christ

They also are to be had accursed that presume to say, that every man shall be saved by the Law or sect which he professeth, so that he be diligent to frame his life according to that Law, and the light of nature. For holy Scripture doth set out unto us only the name of Jesus Christ, whereby men must be saved.

If God's rescue mission is creating the Church by Jesus's sacrifice, there's no other way of being justified, of starting the journey of becoming saved. Though there may be some truth in other religions (because God's preventing or 'prevenient' grace by the Holy Spirit is everywhere, helping everyone somewhat – see Article X), all people need to hear the *Christian* message: It is the only hope that exists. This is the point being made here in Article XVIII.

SESSION 9

Article XIX
Of the Church

The visible Church of Christ is a congregation of faithful men, in which the pure Word of God is preached, and the sacraments be duly ministered according to Christ's ordinance in all those things that of necessity are requisite to the same.

As the Church of Jerusalem, Alexandria, and Antioch, have erred; so also the Church of Rome hath erred, not only in their living and manner of ceremonies, but also in matters of faith.

Look again at that word Cranmer uses in the first line: *visible*. If something is visible, we can see it with our eyes, right? Well, truthfully, the visible church is not exactly same thing as the *real* Church, which consists only of those 'sheep' we talked about in our discussion of Article XVI. Yes, the real Church is that group of people who have been justified (by their faith in Christ) and are being actively prepared by His Spirit: He is slowly changing them like the sea reshapes sharp rocks or jagged glass into smooth, pretty pebbles, for new life in the New Jerusalem in the new earth. This is the invisible Church (with a *big* capital "C," notice), and its boundaries are obvious only to God.

By-and-large, of course, the 'visible church' and the 'invisible Church' overlap:

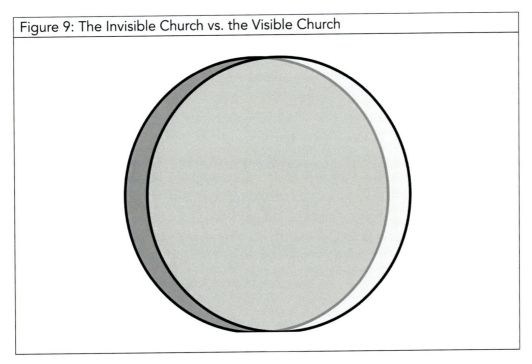

Figure 9: The Invisible Church vs. the Visible Church

However, the overlap is only ever *partial*; they are not exactly one and the same thing, as the circles aren't in the diagram. Indeed, sometimes they are very far apart. For example, on one Friday night, I (Father Ben) visited what looked like a church in Leeds, England. It had beautiful stained-glass windows showing scenes from the Bible and from the lives of various saints. The church was made of grey stone; it had gargoyles (*grrr!*), a cross on a steeple, and so on. When I went inside, however, I discovered it was a nightclub! It was a place with flashing lights and lasers, for dancing and getting drunk on alcohol. *Oops!* (This is a true story.) Clearly, this "church" was not part of the real Church. The people who owned it and the people visiting it were not focused on worshipping God; this wasn't its (or their) purpose.

Every visible church, though, usually has in it a mixture of those being saved (in whom the Holy Spirit is working) and those who are there for different reasons: Maybe it's a child whose mom and dad gave them no choice? Maybe a husband is physically present in the pews because he is trying to please his wife, but his mind is on golf or a football match? —The visible and invisible churches overlap on Sunday mornings, like, as Jesus says, "wheat" and "weeds" often can be found in the same field:

> "Let both grow together until the Harvest. At that time I will tell the workers what to do. Here is what I will say to them. First collect the weeds. Tie them in bundles to be burned. Then gather the wheat. Bring it into my storeroom." (Mt 13:24–30)

By "storeroom," He meant Heaven (the New Jerusalem).

In other words, you and I shouldn't become overly preoccupied trying to figure out the "true" Christians from the "false" ones—God will do that at the General Resurrection (the time of Judgment). You see, when we start scrutinizing others for problems (for their mistakes and foibles), it always leads to trouble! This doesn't mean, however, that we should ignore altogether *glaring* mistakes in our neighbors' behavior or their theology: in *Matthew* 18, Jesus taught that '"If your brother or sister"—another Christian—"sins against you, go to them. Tell them what they did wrong."' (v.15. See also Ezk 33:8.)

In fact, remember the word *heresy*? It is a serious danger to Christians and an obstruction (a barrier) to the Good News (the Gospel), which Jesus commands us all to share. This is why Luther, Cranmer, and other Reformers left the Roman Catholic Church: it "hath erred." That is to say, it was sharing some deeply mistaken ideas—'theology'—not found in the Bible, *and yet* it refused to admit the truth: it was heart-breaking! —they had hoped to *reform* the visible Church, not start (entirely) new ones! But the pope, his friends and allies, just wouldn't listen. Why? That is a *great* question. And the answer is almost certainly…multi-layered. But, basically, we do hear in (the Book of) *Proverbs* that: "The way of foolish people seems right to them." (See 12:15) So, that's part of it. And, sadly, because sometimes being wrong is more profitable in this life than faithfulness. In fact, nearly always.

Article XX
Of the Authority of the Church

The Church hath power to decree rites or ceremonies, and authority in controversies of Faith: And yet it is not lawful for the Church to ordain any thing that is contrary to God's Word written, neither may it so expound one place of Scripture, that it be repugnant to another. Wherefore, although the Church be a witness and a keeper of holy Writ, yet, as it ought not to decree any thing against the same, so besides the same ought it not to enforce any thing to be believed for necessity of salvation.

Cranmer's Tudor English isn't always easy to understand, is it? What's he saying here? Well, I think that what he's saying is this: the top priority (most important job) of the Church (the Elect, those justified by Jesus's sacrifice) is what Jesus commanded as He ascended back to Heaven: "[G]o and make disciples of all nations. Baptize them in the name of the Father and of the Son and of the Holy Spirit. Teach them to obey everything I have commanded you" (Mt 28:19–20a).

In different places and for different people, how we do this will change. In France, for example, it would be silly to tell them about salvation through Christ in Japanese, right? (We're going to talk about this some more when we discuss Article XXIV.) Likewise, the way of worship (its rites or ceremonies) might need to be adapted, adjusted, and reshaped. In fact, here in Article XX, Cranmer says that the Church *should* make the changes that are necessary to help people become Christians. In Islamic countries, for example, the day of rest is Friday. Sunday is a normal day for working at the office, going to school, and so on. It would, then, make sense for us Anglicans to move our main day of worship to Friday if we lived over there. If we didn't, nobody could come!

However, says Cranmer, the Church has no right and no authority to change what is in *the Bible*, or "holy Writ," as he calls it. Why? *Because the Bible belongs to God!* (It is His, not ours.) After all, just imagine you had spent many days carefully making a Lego Star Wars Death Star, a huge model with thousands of little pieces, and then I came to your house and began moving some of the bricks around. Would you be happy? No—you'd be furious, right? Making changes to what it says in the Bible has always been a temptation for Christians to find excuses to make their lives more luxurious, more convenient, and more *selfish.*

The Roman Catholic Church at the time of the Reformation was guilty of doing just this. It misled people about the Gospel, about what God "breathed" and Jesus had taught. In particular, at that time they sold "indulgences" (certificates) to the people of Europe, which, they claimed, would improve a person's situation after death. If you bought a very expensive one, therefore, the Church taught that the punishment for a wicked person's sins would be less severe. In other words, it looked like the justice of God was for sale! —like God accepted bribes. This grotesque mischaracterization was completely unacceptable to Luther, Cranmer, and their friends. God isn't a bully who, if you give Him your lunch money, will agree to leave you alone. Oh no—"God is love" (1 Jn 4:8).

Does that make sense? *"Mischaracterization"* is a long word, right? However, it's a great one so let's learn it. To that end, it might help to illustrate its meaning—literally. Get some paint.

Using your *finger*, not a paintbrush, draw a character (that is, *a face*)—just something simple. You can use more than one color if you like. The key here, however, is to use lots; make thick, sloppy lines, and work quickly. You *don't* want them to dry. Done? Okay. Now, take a clean finger and wipe it back and forth, left and right, across the page, deliberately smudging the portrait. There—it is "mischaracterized." And we must be careful not to do the same when talking about God or *His* Bible.

SESSION 10

Article XXI
Of the Authority of General Councils

General Councils may not be gathered together without the commandment and will of princes. And when they be gathered together, (forasmuch as they be an assembly of men, whereof all be not governed with the Spirit and Word of God,) they may err, and sometimes have erred, even in things pertaining unto God. Wherefore things ordained by them as necessary to salvation have neither strength nor authority, unless it may be declared that they be taken out of Holy Scripture.

Because people make mistakes and mischaracterize God and His plan—with heresy or by ignorance, sometimes on purpose and sometimes not—anything that anybody tells you about Him needs to be double-checked in the Bible. That's *your* responsibility. Even if the vicar or pastor of a church was the one who told you, and even if whole councils (groups) of them seem to agree with one another, *you* must check. And it's okay—a wonderful thing, in fact—to change your mind when you discover something new in a part of the Bible you hadn't read before, or rediscover a lesson—*a truth*— hiding in plain sight in a familiar passage that somehow you'd overlooked. That has happened to me (Father Ben) many, many times over the years. Yes, *whenever* I open the Scriptures, including, to be clear, the Old Testament, I find Jesus waiting for me in its pages, to explain, inspire, and correct me: it's fantastic! Almost a miracle.

Article XXII
Of Purgatory

The Romish doctrine concerning purgatory, pardons, worshipping, and adoration, as well of images as of reliques, and also invocation of saints, is a fond thing vainly invented, and grounded upon no warrant of Scripture, but rather repugnant to the Word of God.

What happens when you die? This may surprise you, but the Bible isn't very clear. In fact, its authors aren't even that interested in the subject. What it *does* say is that when Jesus returns, everyone will be gathered, both those alive at the time and the dead, "to explain their actions to God" (1 Pet 4:5). He will divide them into two groups. (We've talked about this already. Remember? See Article XVI.) One of these groups (those who haven't been justified by Christ and aren't members of the Church) will be "like a branch that…dries up…They are thrown into the fire and burned" (Jn 15:6). That is, they will go to Hell. Everybody else, however, is given—we've learned—an amazing gift of eternal life in a wonderful, remade creation: the new earth, much more beautiful than it is even now.

What happens until then? What happens if I die tonight but Jesus doesn't come back for one thousand years? The most Saint Paul will say is, "I long to leave this world and be with Christ. That is better by far" (Phil 1:23). Usually, however, he says only that the "Intermediate State," which is the time between a person's final breath and the General Resurrection, is like sleeping. (See 1 Cor 15:18.) That's no bad thing, right? I love my bed! It's a cosy, safe place.

Jesus Himself confirms that this is the right way to view death. In (the gospel of) *John*, chapter 11, some visitors come to tell the Savior that His friend Lazarus had died. Jesus, who had decided to bring Lazarus back to life, says this: "'Our friend Lazarus has *fallen asleep*, but I am going there to wake him up.' His disciples replied, 'Lord, if he's sleeping, he will get better.' [But] Jesus had been speaking about the death of Lazarus" (11–12).

Not everyone likes this answer, though. Those who don't sometimes ask, "What about those Christians who confessed their sinfulness (their corruption) and seemed to love Jesus but didn't do a very good job of copying Him, as He said we should? Is there really no second chance?" In response, and taking seriously the focus on deeds (our choices) in God's justice, over time the Roman Catholic Church devised the idea of "Purgatory." This was an idea (*a hope*) they invented that God would continue to help the dead improve, to prepare for Jesus's return even as they lay in their graves. In other words, He would *purge* their souls of any remaining wickedness. And as the years passed, this theology of purgatory became more and more elaborate.

Its most famous portrayal is, you may know, by the Italian poet Dante Alighieri in his work *The Divine Comedy*. This is how he imagined purgatory: as a mountainous island rising sharply from the sea, with "seven realms"[20] or levels, to which the souls of imperfect Christians were brought in a boat driven across the waves by the wings of an angel:

---

[20] Dante Aligheri, *The Divine Comedy of Dante Alighieri: Volume 2: Purgatorio*, ed. Robert M. Durling (Oxford: Oxford University Press, 2003), 23.

"See how he disdains all human means, so that he needs no oars nor any sail but his wings, between shores so distant. See how he has them stretched toward the sky, beating the air with his eternal feathers, that do not change like mortal hairs." Then, as the divine bird came closer and closer to us, it grew brighter, so that my eyes could not sustain it up close, but I lowered them; and he came to shore with a vessel so swift and light that the waters engulfed none of it. At the stern stood the angelic pilot, who seemed to have blessedness inscribed on him; and more than a hundred spirits were sitting within.[21]

Having arrived at the island, these "spirits" are then made to perform various unpleasant tasks as they climb up the mountain toward Heaven. They might carry great, heavy stones on their backs.[22] They might be made to climb with "[their] eyelids pierced and sewn [shut] by an iron wire."[23] These are not easy things to do. Where are the hand-holds? Where should I put my feet? This is the point: these Christians were, in Dante's imagination, being permitted to pay the price for the smaller, post-baptismal sins that we all inevitably commit.

The problem that Reformers like Luther and Cranmer saw with all this was that none of it appears in the Bible. Indeed, the idea of purgatory is actually contradicted in the Bible. Jesus paid it all on the Cross: "We have been set free because of what Christ has done. Because He bled and died, our sins have been forgiven. We have been set free because God's grace is so rich" (Eph 1:7). There is, then, no more "purging" by us to do if we have *truly* put our trust in Him; a human lifetime is enough to make that choice. Thus, as David's son King Solomon taught, "A tree might fall to the south or the north. [But i]t will stay in the place where it falls" (Eccl 11:3). He was speaking metaphorically, with symbols: the "tree" is a person. And what he meant was that the status the person has with God when he or she dies—whether they are Elect or not—is final; it can't be altered.

Finally, notice that purgatory isn't the only false teaching that Article XXII identifies. It also mentions the "worshipping, and adoration…of images [and] reliques, and also [the] invocation of saints."

A "relique"—usually spelled these days as "relic"—is a body-part—a hand, some hair, etc.—or personal belonging of a seemingly *extra* special (holy?) person. They are sometimes proudly displayed in ancient churches, usually around the Mediterranean Sea in countries like Spain and so on.

Once, in fact, when I was a boy and on holiday with my family, I saw one of these "relics" in the city of Siena, Italy. It was the severed head of Saint Catherine! It sits, visible to the public, in a small, ornate case of glass behind the Communion table in the Basilica of San Domenico. Ask your course-leader to search for an image of this on the internet if you're curious. (Or search for it yourself if you've your own smartphone.)

(Pause.)

Creepy, right?

---

[21] Aligheri, 37.
[22] Ibid., 165.
[23] 209.

Now, we might find the example of some saints and their inspiring efforts to be like Christ helpful. Saint Catherine, for example, excelled at self-denial and generosity. She hardly ever spoke. She was wise and trustworthy. She took no delight in her own famed beauty or her family's great wealth; instead she devoted herself to the poor. We all could learn something from her! However, she was still a sinner—a descendent of flawed, fallen Adam like you and me. Honestly, her head has no magical powers. Nonetheless, some Christians ask her or one of the other heroes from history or the Bible (the Virgin Mary, for example) to answer their prayers. And this is a mistake:

> One day Jesus was praying in a certain place. When He finished, one of His disciples spoke to Him: "Lord," he asked, "teach us to pray, just as John [the Baptist] taught his disciples." Jesus said to them, "When you pray, this is what you should say. 'Father, may your name be honored. May your Kingdom come. Give us each day our daily bread. Forgive us our sins, as we also forgive everyone who sins against us. Keep us from falling into sin when we are tempted.'" (Lk 11:1–4).

This passage should sound familiar to you. What do we normally call this prayer—in its longer form, that is?

Answer:

_____

Right! This, then, is the only person we should address our own prayers to: *God.*

Article XXIII
Of Ministering in the Congregation

It is not lawful for any man to take upon him the office of publick preaching, or ministering the Sacraments in the congregation, before he be lawfully called, and sent to execute the same. And those we ought to judge lawfully called and sent, which be chosen and called to this work by men who have publick authority given unto them in the congregation, to call and send ministers into the Lord's vineyard.

The Church is very old. It has seen empires and nations come and go, wars and plagues, and lots and lots of change. However, some things have remained the same: human nature, in particular. And one thing that has happened repeatedly is that there have always been people who decided to start their own 'churches', who declared themselves 'bishops' or 'pastors'. Well, in this Article we see Cranmer saying that no one has the right do this. Rather, preachers, vicars, and the like should be raised up from "[with]in the congregation." We see this in (the Book of) *Acts*.

In the church at Antioch there were prophets and teachers. Among them were Barnabas, Simeon, and Lucius from Cyrene. Simeon was also called Niger. Another was Manaen. He had been brought up with Herod, the ruler of Galilee. Saul was among them too. While they were worshiping the Lord and fasting, the Holy Spirit spoke. "Set apart Barnabas and Saul for me," He said. "I have appointed them to do special work." The prophets and teachers fasted and prayed. They placed their hands on Barnabas and Saul. Then they sent them off. (13:1–3)

This is how we should do it today; it is our *precedent*, our example. We should be wary (suspicious), therefore, of anybody who does the opposite.

Article XXIV
Of Speaking in the Congregation in Such a Tongue as the People Understandeth

It is a thing plainly repugnant to the Word of God, and the custom of the primitive Church, to have publick prayer in the Church, or to minister the Sacraments in a tongue not understanded of the people.

Imagine yourself standing at the airport, waiting for a plane. Suddenly, you hear a voice over the speakers in the terminal announcing which gate is for your flight, but they give the information you need in a *foreign* language—one you don't understand! What would you do? Panic, right? *"Ah! Where do I go? Who can help me?"* Well, for many, many years, the Church in Europe (before America was discovered) used only Latin, the language of the ancient Romans, and in the Middle East, Greek. However, most people didn't speak either. They were Germans or French or Arabs. They had no idea what the preacher was saying in the pulpit, or when the minister was presiding at the Eucharist. This was a serious problem. Presumably, he was offering them "the words of eternal life" (Jn 6:68), but they couldn't be *sure*. The Reformers, therefore, worked hard to make available religious materials that people could read themselves, such as *The Book of Common Prayer* in which we find the Thirty-Nine Articles. It was released by Cranmer in March 1549 and distributed, at great expense, to churches throughout England. (Printing, you see, was a very tricky thing to do back then. They used a piece of hard-to-build, heavy machinery called a "press.") And do you know what happened? Riots broke out; there was fighting in the streets! Mobs tore up copies of *The Book of Common Prayer* and burned them in big fires, especially in Cornwall.[24] Young King Edward VI, however, intervened and passed a law through Parliament saying everyone had to use the book when they gathered for worship. This was the 'Act of Uniformity'.

---

24 Barrett L. Beer, *Rebellion and Riot: Popular Disorder in England During the Reign of Edward VI* (Kent, OH: The Kent State University Press, 2005), 38f.

Article XXV
Of the Sacraments

Sacraments ordained of Christ be not only badges or tokens of Christian men's profession, but rather they be certain sure witnesses, and effectual signs of grace, and God's good will towards us, by the which he doth work invisibly in us, and doth not only quicken, but also strengthen and confirm our Faith in him.

There are two sacraments ordained of Christ our Lord in the Gospel, that is to say, baptism, and the "Supper of the Lord."

Those five commonly called "Sacraments," that is to say, confirmation, penance, orders, matrimony, and extreme unction, are not to be counted for sacraments of the Gospel, being such as have grown partly of the corrupt following of the Apostles, partly are states of life allowed in the Scriptures; but yet have not like nature of sacraments with baptism, and the Lord's Supper, for that they have not any visible sign or ceremony ordained of God.

The sacraments were not ordained of Christ to be gazed upon, or to be carried about, but that we should duly use them. And in such only as worthily receive the same they have a wholesome effect or operation: but they that receive them unworthily purchase to themselves damnation, as Saint Paul saith.

In our discussion of Article XXIV, I mentioned that there was some violence and trouble when Cranmer first released *The Book of Common Prayer*. That's because it was "a revolution in religious practice."[25] It set in motion, like a stone that rolls down a hill, moving faster and faster, big changes in the way medieval people worshipped. It was "the domino of personal, communal, and national transformations."[26] And, often, people (you and me) don't react well to sudden change. We tend to react against it even if it is good for us, like leaning *away* from a doctor as he approaches with a needle (to vaccinate us against a deadly disease). Others, however, eagerly welcomed the Reformation as a necessary 'course-correction': England, then, was divided. Her population was polarized between two (different) 'camps'. —those whose worship and theology continued to be Roman Catholic, and those practicing the new Protestantism, which found its voice in the Articles. And these two positions have in many ways and contexts continued to diverge, becoming *more* distinct, *particularly* in regard to their use of something Cranmer calls the "Sacraments."

A 'sacrament'—a word that first came up *way* back in Session 1—refers to an action carried out in the Church when Christians are gathered together in worship "to encourage and strengthen them."[27] They are almost like small bits of theatre—like a single scene from a play, and "[b]y our use of them the Holy Spirit more fully declares and seals the promises of the Gospel to us."[28]

---

[25] Brian Cummings, "Introduction," in *The Book of Common Prayer: The Texts of 1549, 1559, and 1662* (Oxford: Oxford University Press, 2011), xiii.

[26] Ibid., xiii.

[27] The Gospel Coalition, *The New City Catechism: Curriculum—Volume 3: Spirit, Restoration, Growing in Grace, Questions 36-52* (Wheaton, IL: Crossway, 2018), 72

[28] The Gospel Coalition and Redeemer Presbyterian Church, *The New City Catechism: 52 Questions and Answers for our Hearts and Minds* (Wheaton, IL: Crossway, 2017), 105.

Now, Protestants (that's us—those who think the Reformation was a good and necessary thing) properly recognize two:

1. Baptism; and
2. The Eucharist, also called Communion or the Lord's Supper.

That's because these small bits of theatre are re-enactments of things that Jesus Himself performed and commanded. That is to say, they are "dominical." (*Domus* in Latin means "Lord.") Roman Catholic Christians, however, and the Oriental Churches, add five others. Their performance of the Sacraments tends to be a little more elaborate, more…showy: Yes, the wafer or bread of Communion, for example, is sometimes displayed in their churches for a time before being eaten. It is placed in something called a "monstrance;" displayed like an expensive jewel or an artwork in a museum. It is also paraded back and forth for people to admire. This is why Cranmer says, "The sacraments were not ordained of Christ to be gazed upon, or to be carried about, but that we should duly use them." In other words, "Just eat it," he says. That's what it's for.

Of course, the split among English/European Christians was never what Jesus wanted for His justified people, the Elect. Edward VI's sister, Queen Elizabeth I, tried hard to mend the split, and we must too! Let's pray as Jesus prayed: "'Father, I pray they will be one, just as you are in me and I am in you. I want them also to be in us. Then the world will believe that you have sent me'" (Jn 17:21).

Article XXVI
Of the Unworthiness of the Ministers, Which Hinders Not the Effect of the Sacrament

Although in the visible Church the evil be ever mingled with the good, and sometimes the evil have chief authority in the ministration of the Word and Sacraments, yet forasmuch as they do not the same in their own name, but in Christ's, and do minister by His commission and authority, we may use their ministry, both in hearing the Word of God, and in receiving of the sacraments. Neither is the effect of Christ's ordinance taken away by their wickedness, nor the grace of God's gifts diminished from such as by faith and rightly do receive the sacraments ministered unto them; which be effectual, because of Christ's institution and promise, although they be ministered by evil men.

Nevertheless, it appertaineth to the discipline of the Church, that inquiry be made of evil Ministers, and that they be accused by those that have knowledge of their offences; and finally being found guilty, by just judgement be deposed.

The two sacraments, Baptism and the Eucharist, are special. They're special because Jesus Himself thought they were special. They seem to have *real* power. Here, in this Article, Cranmer reassures us that that "power" is not dependant on the person (the vicar or pastor) who offers them. The Lord's Supper (Communion), for example, which reminds us of how Jesus's body was broken on the Cross to justify sinners who repent, is a great comfort to those Christians who eat it. That comfort they feel, from the knowledge that their sins have been washed away, comes from the Holy Spirit, not from the person who gave them the bread.

SESSION 12

Article XXVII
Of Baptism

What happens at a baptism? Do you know?

Answer:

_____

_____

_____

Okay! We do this strange thing because Jesus commanded that it was necessary for His followers (see Mt 28:19). But what does it mean? Cranmer explains it here.

> *Baptism is not only a sign of profession, and mark of difference, whereby Christian men are discerned from others that be not christened, but it is also a sign of regeneration or new birth, whereby, as by an instrument, they that receive baptism rightly are grafted into the Church; the promises of forgiveness of sin, and of our adoption to be the sons of God by the Holy Ghost, are visibly signed and sealed; Faith is confirmed, and grace increased by virtue of prayer unto God. The baptism of young children is in any wise to be retained in the Church, as most agreeable with the institution of Christ.*

In other words, as we said earlier, the Sacraments have a *power*. And in this Article Cranmer explains the 'power' and purpose of *baptism*: As Martin Davie says, it "gives the person baptized God's gift of new life, but in order to be fruitful this gift has to be received and the way it is received is through repentance and faith."[29] Does that make sense? No? Okay, let's keep this simple. Do you remember the diagram of sheep entering a sheepfold when we discussed Article XVI? Well, baptism is, to use Cranmer's word, the "instrument" by which we join the Elect, the justified people being set apart for the New Jerusalem in the new earth when Jesus returns. That opportunity is available only because Jesus paid the entrance fee and opened the door by His death. We receive that gift by sincerely confessing—knowing—our need of it; we receive it 'by faith'. Baptism, then, is like the moving walkway (at the airport) that takes us *in*.

---

[29] Martin Davie, *Our Inheritance of Faith: A Commentary on the Thirty Nine Articles* (West Knapton, UK: Gilead Books Publishing, 2019), 493.

Wait, what? A 'moving walkway'? Yes: "baptism is more than a mere symbol... baptism [i]s a *vehicle for the conveyance of grace*."[30] For those for whom *God* intends it to function that way, of course; which is (only) those men and women, *boys and girls*, that God *predestined* to respond appropriately (with gratitude) to the Gospel—*with faith*. This entails two things:

1. "The [genuinely) baptized cannot become unbaptized;"[31] it's a one-time thing. It can't be repeated, but it can be *affirmed*. That is to say, a person might find it helpful to repeat *the process* of undergoing *the rite* of baptism.

2. If we get our theology right, *infant* baptism makes *perfect* sense, (which is why Cranmer and *all* the Reformers encouraged the practice). Why? Because those who receive the gift of faith are already foreknown to the LORD: their age at the time they commence the journey of salvation is insignificant—as much as their skin-color or their gender or *their sinfulness*. Thus, Jesus says: "*Let the little children come to me. Don't keep them away.*" —see *Matthew* 19:14. (My emphasis.) Now, admittedly, this passage is not *specifically* about the matter of baptism, but it certainly applies. As does the incident in the chapter before where Jesus sat a child—in Greek: a '*micron*'—on His knee and said that that child could indeed enter "the Kingdom;" they didn't have to *do* anything. God's sacraments *will* be effective for His sheep; His Elect. *He* guarantees it, whether they have the maturity or wisdom to actually articulate and declare their beliefs or not. They will, of course, have to at some point: see Article XI 'Of the Justification of Humankind'. But until they reach that juncture their saving conviction is like a seed hiding in their hearts, planted by supernatural means: as King David put it in one of his psalms—

    "You made me trust in you *even when I was at my mother's breast*. (...) Ever since I came out of my mother's body, you have been my God."
    (22:9b-10, my emphasis.)

Now, since *we* can't be sure who are the 'sheep', upon whom the Good Shepherd (that is, God), has placed His "seal" (2 Cor 1:22), the Church; the *new* Israel, ought to bring every child for baptism, therefore, without delay, trusting that they *are* 'set apart' for citizenship in the New Jerusalem; that they will be counted among His 'flock' on the Last Day! —exactly as the Hebrews—*old* Israel—circumcised all *their* children: it was a sign of hope, you see—that every Jewish boy would grow "more and more pleasing to the LORD" (1 Sam 2:26), proving themselves His worthy sons by the Spirit. But we know, of course, that many didn't: just recall, for instance, any of the many disappointing (*dreadful!*) kings of Judah, like Manasseh, Ahaz, Jehoiakim, etc., etc. These men were all circumcised (as babies), but as Paul explains: "if you break the law, it is just as if you hadn't been circumcised." (Rom 2:25) That is to say, if you are grossly (very, continually) unfaithful to God, what you are doing is showing your 'true colors'—that "You belong to [another] father[, that is], the Devil." (Jn 8:44. See also 1 Jn 3:8. And see too: Gal 3:7.)

---

[30] See: *Report for the Special Committee Appointed by the Council on the Question of Union between Baptists, Congregationalists and Presbyterians* (London: Baptist Union, 1937), 28-29

[31] Colin Buchanan, *A Case for Infant Baptism* (Cambridge, UK: Grove Books, Ltd., 2009), 7. (If you're unconvinced about the case I've briefly made here for baptizing babies, I recommend reading Buchanan's book in its entirety. And not just this one, see also: Douglas Wilson, *To a Thousand Generations: Infant Baptism—Covenant Mercy for the People of God* (Moscow, ID: Canon Press, 1996).)

Article XXVIII
Of the Lord's Supper

The "Supper of the Lord" is not only a sign of the love that Christians ought to have among themselves one to another; but rather is a Sacrament of our redemption by Christ's death: insomuch that to such as rightly, worthily, and with faith, receive the same, the bread which we break is a partaking of the body of Christ; and likewise the cup of blessing is a partaking of the blood of Christ.

Transubstantiation (or the change of the substance of bread and wine) in the Supper of the Lord, cannot be proved by holy Writ; but is repugnant to the plain words of Scripture, overthroweth the nature of a Sacrament, and hath given occasion to many superstitions.

The body of Christ is given, taken, and eaten, in the Supper, only after an heavenly and spiritual manner. And the mean whereby the body of Christ is received and eaten in the Supper is Faith.

The Sacrament of the Lord's Supper was not by Christ's ordinance reserved, carried about, lifted up, or worshipped.

Article XXVIII is the first in a series of four Articles that deal with the Eucharist, also called 'the Lord's Supper' or 'Holy Communion'. Just as we learned in our discussion about Article XXVI (that baptism has a power or efficacy), this one does too!

For the longest time—though not at first—Christians thought that the bread and wine actually became Jesus's body and blood at the moment of consecration, even though both things continued to look unchanged. After all, when Jesus performed the first Eucharist, He did say, "This is my body" and "This is my blood." (See Mt 26:26b–28.) Of course, He also frequently spoke in

metaphors (poetically). Furthermore, He Himself was sitting there when those words were spoken. He was *using* His body and blood to breathe and talk and share that Last Supper. Finally, Jesus is still using His body and blood at this very moment in Heaven, which is where He ascended after the Resurrection. With these facts in mind, the Reformers realized that Jesus could not have been speaking in a literal sense. However, the old way of believing was hard to leave behind.

Cranmer, for example, was first converted to Protestantism by followers of Luther. He was not converted by Luther himself, to be precise: Luther was hiding in Wartburg Castle in Eisenach—remember? (See Article XIII.) No, the main person who convinced Cranmer about the theological truths being rediscovered during the Reformation was called, "Andreas Osiander."

Cranmer and Osiander met in Nuremberg, which is another city in Germany. Cranmer was there to meet with the Holy Roman Emperor (a very powerful king—the most powerful king in Europe, in fact, at that time) to ask him to intimidate (that is, *to bully*) the pope in Rome, who was refusing to grant Cranmer's king, Henry VIII, a divorce. The pope was refusing to do that because, among other reasons, Jesus taught that marriage is very precious to God, and divorce ought always to be avoided apart from the most extreme circumstances: see *Matthew 19:1-12*.

Lutherans, however, like Osiander, though they had many important, *biblical* criticisms of the theology of medieval Roman Catholicism, continued to agree with Roman Catholics about the Eucharistic bread and the wine transforming, *literally*, into Jesus. It was another man, a devoted student of the Scriptures, who probably deserves the credit for explaining to Cranmer how this was also a mistake. That man was Martin Bucer.

Bucer was from Switzerland, but he taught at the University of Cambridge in England. He was widely admired and respected for being very, very wise. And what he showed to Cranmer was this: in Communion we experience "a *spiritual* presence of Christ that [i]s *not* simply identical with the presence imparted by faith at other moments in life."[32] That *real* "presence" can *change* you, and it can *charge* you—for the week ahead, like a battery: the effect (the result) depends on *you* and on your frame of mind; your attitude when you take the sacrament. Really, then, what it comes down to is this: are you sincerely grateful, when you take that little wafer in your hand, for what Jesus suffered? Does the thought of Him—the Lord of lords, "God of God, light of light"—'substituting' Himself in your place on the Cross make you "tremble, tremble" when you think about it? —like in the words of that song, *Were You There When They Crucified My Lord?* Because it should. That's the *key*.

---

[32] Peter Brooks, *Thomas Cranmer's Doctrine of the Eucharist: An Essay in Historical Development* (London: MacMillan and Co., Ltd., 1965), 64–65.

Article XXIX
Of the Wicked Which Eat Not the Body of Christ in the Use of the Lord's Supper

The wicked, and such as be void of a lively faith, although they do carnally and visibly press with their teeth (as Saint Augustine saith) the Sacrament of the body and blood of Christ, yet in no wise are they partakers of Christ: but rather, to their condemnation, do eat and drink the sign or Sacrament of so great a thing.

Because the Eucharist is such a deeply important thing, and since it symbolizes the most important thing that ever happened (Jesus dying on the Cross), it needs protection to preserve its preciousness. This is why Cranmer here teaches that people who have refused to ask God for His forgiveness for their sins should not be allowed to eat it—or, as we see he says (above), "press [it] with their teeth."

Of course, having said this, what Cranmer didn't imagine or intend was that we would stop and intimidate each person who came forward at the time to receive Communion, to interrogate them about their personal lives, before allowing them to receive the sacramental bread and wine. After all, anyone who volunteered to be "Communion Police" would be a hypocrite, right? Do you know that word? A *hypocrite* is someone who tells others how they should behave but doesn't actually behave that way himself or herself. Jesus had a stern warning for such people: "'Do not judge other people. Then you will not be judged. You will be judged in the same way you judge others. You will be measured in the same way you measure others'" (Mt 7:1–2).

What Jesus didn't teach, however, was that we should never criticize someone who we see doing something obviously wrong—something that displeases God and goes against His design: (see our discussion of Article XIX). He Himself did that many times when He was here on earth in Judea/Palestine. Therefore, when we do have a criticism of another person we must offer it to him or her *with love*, or not at all.

In other words, we *should* criticize, but like Jesus. (See 1 Pet 2:21.) So, to be precise, we should speak gently using carefully chosen words, and only when we are certain we have all the facts. I hope you agree that the right time and place to do this properly is not in the middle of the sanctuary (nave) during a worship service or at the Communion rail. Speak to them later, or ideally *before*, when the criticism can be kept "between the two of you" (Mt 18:15).

Article XXX
Of Both Kinds

The cup of the Lord is not to be denied to the lay-people: for both the parts of the Lord's Sacrament, by Christ's ordinance and commandment, ought to be ministered to all Christian men alike.

Because the Eucharist is precious, it is performed with a number of unusual and exotic items that you don't see anywhere but in church. Do you know all their names?

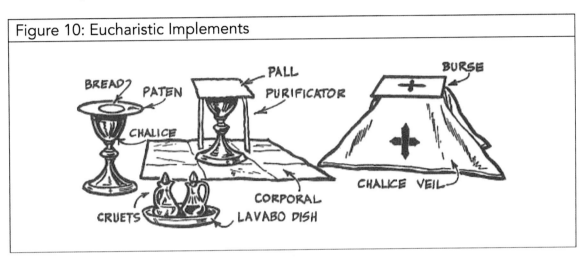

Figure 10: Eucharistic Implements

Of course, these items aren't essential. Really, a minister needs only the bread, wine, and one other person to share them with. But is that glorifying God? To *glorify* someone is to make him or her feel or look good. Should we do better than just the minimum for the LORD if we can? After all, imagine I gave you a birthday gift and didn't bother to wrap it. Now imagine that it was wrapped in thick, shiny, metallic paper and finished with a bold, bright bow. What would you prefer? Does one method of presentation show more care or less? Does one method of presentation show more or less love? I think you know the answer, which is why the best Anglican worship is beautiful and dignified.

Article XXXI
Of the One Oblation of Christ Finished upon the Cross

The offering of Christ once made is that perfect redemption, propitiation, and satisfaction, for all the sins of the whole world, both original and actual; and there is none other satisfaction for sin, but that alone. Wherefore the "sacrifices" of masses, in the which it was commonly said, that the priest did offer Christ for the quick and the dead, to have remission of pain or guilt, were blasphemous fables, and dangerous deceits.

Mass is the name given to Holy Communion (a. k. a., the Lord's Supper) by Roman Catholic Christians. In their theology, when the minister at the front performs the sacrament, they think the minister (the priest) actually sacrifices Jesus *again* for the sins of the whole world, that He is being murdered again and again, over and over. Such an idea mischaracterizes what the Bible itself claims about what happened on the Cross; He did it "once and for all time" (Heb 10:10). That's what makes it so amazing! It doesn't matter how many people were born and sinned after Jesus died, His love, the gift of new, abundant life with Him, is enough. This is why Jesus Himself described what happened as a "spring of water" that keeps on gushing forever, giving salvation to everyone who wants it, whenever they want it. (See Jn 4:13–14.) This is why, perhaps, it is important to offer and receive Communion frequently (at least once a week) to symbolize how Jesus's forgiveness is always available to anyone until the end of time. We can never run out of it. It is there waiting when you go looking for it.

Article XXXII
Of the Marriage of Priests

Bishops, priests, and deacons, are not commanded by God's Law, either to vow the estate of single life, or to abstain from marriage: therefore it is lawful for them, as for all other Christian men, to marry at their own discretion, as they shall judge the same to serve better to godliness.

Jesus, though Himself unmarried, never told His followers to do the same. But by the early fourth-century A.D., the Church in western Europe was requiring that 'priests' and 'bishops'—Christian leaders, that is—*should* copy His singleness. Why? Well, to be blunt, the Church became "intoxicated by Greek attitudes toward sexual repression."[33] That is to say, Christians were influenced in their thinking about this topic by *pagan* ideas absorbed from the world in which they lived and worked. Specifically, Christian theology was distorted by a philosophy called, 'Neopythagoreanism', which *hated* the "very good" flesh God chose to make. (See Gen 1:31)

Furthermore, the Apostle Paul in his first letter to the young congregation in Corinth did say: "I speak now to those who are not married. I also speak to widows. It is good for you to stay single like me" (7:8–9). Why would he say such a thing?! Well, it is argued that a bachelor (a man without a family) has more time to devote to the Church. After all, there are only so many hours in the day! But then maybe this is precisely *why* a wife might be useful? —as a partner. In fact, John Calvin, one of the leading Reformers after Martin Luther, said about his own wife that she was not only "the best companion of my life" but "she was the faithful helper of my ministry."[34]

Anyway, Paul certainly wasn't against marriage: he *was* married. That is to say, he *had* been—we believe. But his wife presumably died before his conversion to Christianity whilst he was still a *pharisee*. To be a 'pharisee', you see, it would have been unthinkable, outrageous, *disqualifying* to be unmarried; to refrain from being…'fruitful'.[35] After all, that was the *very* first thing God said when He created humanity: "Have children." (See Gen 1:28) And, accordingly, *all* the most ancient heroes in the Old Testament—the 'patriarchs' (Noah, Abraham, etc.)—had great, *big* families.

The truth is, Jesus calls on each of us to put Him—and thus His *people*, the Church—*first*, above all other things, including our personal plans, ambitions, *and romance.* "'No one can serve two masters'," He said (Mt 6:24). However, marriage is the *very* place where we learn, practice, and perfect loving others—our "neighbors"—as ourselves: (see Lev 19:18 & Mt 22:39). With a wife or a husband we begin to *truly* do as the early Christians did: "they shared everything they owned" (*Acts* 4:32). And whenever *we* do this, it glorifies God and allows the world a glimpse of His Kingdom, which is "drawing near." The marriage of committed disciples, therefore, can be a very powerful force for change. In fact, to his young friend "Titus," Paul actually *recommends* that Christian leaders *should* have a spouse—just the one, mind; and children—polite, obedient children, that is! (See: Tit 1:5-6.)

---

[33] William E. Phipps, *Clerical Celibacy: The Heritage* (New York, NY: Continuum, 2004), 89.

[34] As quoted in Steven Ozment, *The Age of Reform, 1250-1550: An Intellectual and Religious History of Late Medieval and Reformation Europe* (New Haven, CT: Yale University Press, 2020), 392.

[35] See: Denny Burk, "Was the Apostle Paul Married?" Available at https://www.dennyburk.com/was-the-apostle-paul-married/, (accessed May 1, 2024). Also: Harvey McArthur, "Celibacy in Judaism at the Time of Christian Beginnings," *Andrews University Seminary Studies* 25, No. 2 (1987): pp. 163-181.

Article XXXIII
Of Excommunicate Persons, How They Are to Be Avoided

Titus wasn't Paul's only friend; there was also Timothy. To Timothy, Paul wrote, "[God] wants all people to be saved." It doesn't matter what their skin color is or where they were born. It doesn't matter if they think they belong to another religion or what they did in the past. "He wants them to come to know the truth: There is only one God. And there is only one go-between for God and human beings. He is the man Christ Jesus. He gave himself to pay for the sins of all people" (1 Tim 2:3–6a). The Church is where those people—*Christians*—gather to learn from the Bible together and help and encourage each other; to be *sanctified* (made more holy) together as they wait and prepare for the Last Day and Judgment.

The Church, in other words, is a bit like a school—a 'school' for *holiness*, that is. But, as we've already observed in our discussion about 'sheep' and 'goats' (see Article XVI), there will always be 'students' who attend on a Sunday yet don't really believe the amazing claims preached from the pulpit. Because they haven't the Spirit. Because the 'Good News' is, let's face it, rather *incredible!* But, occasionally, there will be those in the pews who've no intention whatsoever of changing their minds or being persuaded. In fact, they might actually seek to *sabotage* the Church and cause confusion. In (a normal) school, these 'students'—the insistently naughty ones—are put in detention, right? Well, the Church has its own form of detention too: excommunication. That's what Article XXXIII is about. Cranmer says,

> *That person which by open denunciation of the Church is rightly cut off from the unity of the Church, and excommunicated, ought to be taken of the whole multitude of the faithful, as an heathen and publican, until he be openly reconciled by penance, and received into the Church by a judge that hath authority thereunto.*

In other words, an excommunicated person should be put in a "time out" by their friends and neighbors until they say, "Sorry" and *repent*. It's for their own good! It is these excommunicated people that Cranmer had in mind when he said, in Article XXIX, that some shouldn't be allowed to "press with their teeth" (eat) Communion.

Article XXXIV
Of the Traditions of the Church

A little while ago, when we discussed Article XX, we heard how "the way of worship [in church]" (its "rites or ceremonies") might need adaptation; to be adjusted and reshaped over time and in different places to help people hear and respond to the Gospel. Cranmer emphasizes the point again here in this Article:

It is not necessary that traditions and ceremonies be in all places one, and utterly like; for at all times they have been diverse, and may be changed according to the diversities of countries, times, and men's manners, so that nothing be ordained against God's Word. Whosoever through his private judgement, willingly and purposely, doth openly break the traditions and ceremonies of the Church, which be not repugnant to the Word of God, and be ordained and approved by common authority, ought to be rebuked openly, (that others may fear to do the like,) as he that offendeth against the common order of the Church, and hurteth the authority of the magistrate, and woundeth the consciences of the weak brethren.

Every particular or national Church hath authority to ordain, change, and abolish, ceremonies or rites of the Church ordained only by man's authority, so that all things be done to edifying.

Why does it matter for the Church to be ready to change its music, the clothes of the minister, the style of the building, and so on? Because nothing—*nothing(!)*—is more important than finding salvation (abundant life) through Jesus Christ. And yet the reality is that people are easily distracted by the wrong things; that is, by *trivial* things.

Imagine offering a person who was really thirsty a drink, but the glass it is in has some big, nasty-looking cracks. The person might worry that those cracks would cut his or her lips if he or she tried to drink from that glass, and so the person refuses your help. That would be silly, perhaps, but you can imagine someone doing that, can't you? Or imagine a fantastic story but the book it is written in had a dirty, stained cover. You wouldn't pick it up to read, would you? Well, a church that refuses to think about its appearance or to adapt (change) its presentation of the Gospel is one that fails to glorify God.

(See over.)

Review Session 1

We're almost finished! This means that we've learned a lot together to prepare you for a big step in your relationship with Jesus, whatever that is. Maybe it is putting your faith in Him? Or deciding to be baptized? Or maybe it is being confirmed and/or receiving Holy Communion for the first time? Either way, let's test ourselves a little.

1. The thing we've been learning from the Thirty-Nine Articles is correct *theology*. That's from the Greek. What did I say it means?

    _____

    _____

2. We've learned that there's a difference between good theology and bad theology. Good theology uses the Bible, a unique collection of books the writing of which was inspired by God. How many books are there in the Old Testament? (Clue: the answer is at the end of Session 5.)

    _____

    _____

3. Sometimes, the Bible and God are "mischaracterized" by people, even by Christians. What does that word mean?

    _____

    _____

4. For a very long time, the Roman Catholic Church was guilty of some bad theology. In the sixteenth century (about 500 years ago), a few brave men and women rebelled. They said, "Enough!" This very, very important moment was called The

    R_____

5. The new type of Christianity, which arose from that excitement, is known as Protestantism. (To *protest* is to point out that something is wrong in the world.) Anglicans (or Episcopalians) belong to this group. Is that true? Check a box.

    Yes: ☐
    No: ☐

SESSION 14

Article XXXV
Of the Homilies

The second "Book of Homilies," the several titles whereof we have joined under this Article, doth contain a godly and wholesome doctrine, and necessary for these times, as doth the former "Book of Homilies," which were set forth in the time of Edward the VI; and therefore we judge them to be read in churches by the ministers, diligently and distinctly, that they may be understanded of the people.

Preaching a sermon every week isn't always easy. Sometimes the Holy Spirit is like, *Blam! Whoosh*, and an idea comes straight into my (that is, Father Ben's) head. However, there are other times when I'm just…stuck—stuck scratching my head for hours. (After all, the Bible can be a tricky book to understand in a few places.) Well, to help ministers in Tudor England, Cranmer wrote not only these Thirty-Nine Articles we've been discussing; he also wrote a whole book of sermons. He calls them, "The Homilies." They're like a cheat-sheet—a short cut. We all need one of those sometimes, don't we?

Article XXXVI
Of the Consecration of Bishops and Ministers

The Book of Consecration of archbishops and bishops, and Ordering of Priests and Deacons, lately set forth in the time of Edward the VI, and confirmed at the same time by authority of parliament, doth contain all things necessary to such consecration and ordering: neither hath it any thing, that of itself is superstitious and ungodly. And therefore whosoever are consecrated or ordered according to the rites of that book, since the second year of the forenamed King Edward unto this time, or hereafter shall be consecrated or ordered according to the same rites; we decree all such to be rightly, orderly, and lawfully consecrated and ordered.

Earlier, in our discussion of Article XXVIII, we discovered that Thomas Cranmer, (the main) author of the Thirty-Nine Articles (and the *Book of Common Prayer*), was converted to Protestantism—that's our version of Christianity, remember—by meeting friends of Martin Luther in Germany. We learned too that he had gone there (to that country) as an ambassador of King Henry VIII of England, who was seeking the permission of the pope, a man called 'Clement VII', to divorce. —and for good reason: Henry's wife Catherine had been married to his brother! And that was something forbidden in the Bible: see *Leviticus* 20:21. And yet the pope refused; he refused even though other kings *had* been granted divorces.

Now it probably didn't help that when Cranmer first met Clement, the pope stuck out his foot for him to kneel and kiss, but he declined. And it was *very…*awkward! The pope just kept sitting there, waiting, his pampered foot in a velvet slipper raised up in the air. And then suddenly a dog belonging to a man in Cranmer's entourage; to Thomas Boleyn, the Earl of Wiltshire, sprang forward and bit it! *Grrr(!)*, crunch: yes, the dog—a little spaniel—bit the pope's toes!

Anyway, Henry got mad. He got *sooo* mad that Clement wouldn't give him what he wanted (he hoped to marry Boleyn's pretty daughter, Anne, you see), that he decided to separate the Church in England from the pope's control: All the priests and the bishops in his kingdom would now have to do what *he* said and follow *his* rules. And, oh dear! This doesn't sound very good, does it? (Not really, no.) But it *is* sometimes said that 'God moves in mysterious ways', and, sure enough, Henry's temper-tantrum turned out to be a very, *very* good thing indeed: It allowed Reformation theology (*true* theology and right thinking based on the Bible) to advance and flourish among English-speaking people everywhere, which the popes and their subordinates had been suppressing.

However, some of the priests and the bishops worried. They worried that if the pope was no longer the boss, their ordinations were no longer valid or *real*. (To be *ordained* is to become a professional minister in the Church, one who is paid and entrusted to preach sermons, lead worship, and preside at the Eucharist.) Cranmer, their new leader (on Henry's behalf) as the *Arch*bishop, told them to "relax." (My word!) They could "relax" because the chain of ordination (of priests and bishops making other priests and bishops) began with the Twelve Apostles themselves—the *original* disciples (like Peter), choosing and laying hands on the heads of those they wanted to lead the Church after they were dead and gone. And that "chain" remained unbroken. So, although Henry was in charge and not the pope anymore, (and after Henry, his son, Edward, and then Queen Elizabeth, and so on), no one could take back the Holy Spirit given to holy, Jesus-loving men at their ordination. And that's true still today.

Article XXXVII
Of the Civil Magistrates

The King's majesty hath the chief power in this realm of England, and other his dominions, unto whom the chief government of all estates of this realm, whether they be ecclesiastical or civil, in all causes doth appertain, and is not, nor ought to be, subject to any foreign jurisdiction. Where we attribute to the king's majesty the chief government, by which titles we understand the minds of some slanderous folks to be offended; we give not to our princes the ministering either of God's Word, or of the sacraments, the which thing the injunctions also lately set forth by Elizabeth our Queen do most plainly testify; but that only prerogative, which we see to have been given always to all godly princes in the holy Scriptures by God himself; that is, that they should rule all estates and degrees committed to their charge by God, whether they be Ecclesiastical or Temporal, and restrain with the civil sword the stubborn and evil-doers.

The Bishop of Rome hath no jurisdiction in this realm of England.

The laws of the realm may punish Christian men with death, for heinous and grievous offences.

It is lawful for Christian men, at the commandment of the magistrate, to wear weapons, and serve in the wars.

In this Article, we hear Cranmer saying some of those things I just described about King Henry putting himself in charge of the Church in England and removing it from the authority of the papacy. This wasn't a perfect arrangement by any means: oh no! But what *was* clear to Cranmer was that the pope, *as a priest*, had obviously gained more political power than the Bible said he should have. It was grotesque, actually: the papacy had itself become an idol; an obstacle; a… false 'god'.

According to the Bible, you see, because of our fallenness (which we've talked about already in this course: see Articles II and IX), one person shouldn't have too much control or authority over other people. One person can't be trusted with it. *Yet* also because of our fallenness (our corrupt, sinful wills) we need bosses (people, that is, whose job it is to make rules and make sure the rules are followed). This seems like a paradox, right? Well, thankfully in the Old Testament we find a timeless model of how power can—and ought to—be *divided* in any community of persons: *between* kings, priests, and prophets, (or whatever their nearest, modern equivalent is—i.e., between the president, your pastor, a judge, and so on). Each is a different type of boss that Christians should respect, and to whom we should submit. (See: Rom 13:4–5; Heb 13:17; and 2 Chron 20:20, for instance.)

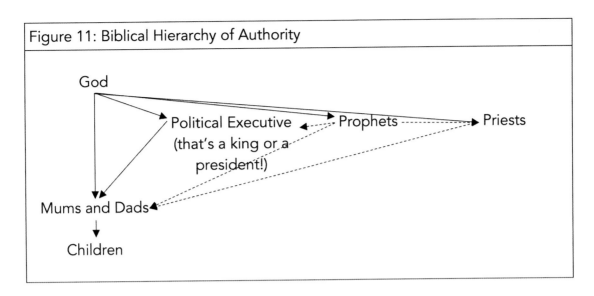

Figure 11: Biblical Hierarchy of Authority

Being king or queen is a lot of responsibility—like being president or a governor of a state in America. The choices they make have real consequences for many people, namely, their subjects. This is why Saint Paul says, "Pray for kings. Pray for everyone who is in authority. Pray that we can live peaceful and quiet lives" (1 Tim 2:2a). In fact, it is the first duty (the priority) of the government to make sure that the country is calm, peaceful, and orderly. As Saint Augustine observed in his huge book *The City of God*, this is the best condition for Christians like you and me to share the Gospel about Christ and Him crucified.

After all, if the roads and public places are full of murderers and thieves, we will be too scared to leave our homes to tell our friends and neighbors about the love of God, and the need to repent and say sorry to Him. To prevent murderers and thieves from causing a big mess, therefore, God expects us sometimes, as Cranmer teaches, "to wear weapons, and serve in the wars." *That's right!* We *may* use violence—in very, very rare circumstances, that is. However, didn't Jesus tell us to "turn the other cheek"? (Mt 5:39) He did. He wants us to trust Him and His promise of eternal life in the New Jerusalem in the new earth *sooo(!)* much that we won't worry about defending our own lives against danger. After all, if there really is a better place coming after the General Resurrection and Judgment Day, as the Bible teaches, then it wouldn't be right to hurt someone else, even an enemy, just so I can enjoy a few more hours or years in a creation, which, in the end, will be replaced by something far, far better.

Jesus, however, also told us to love our neighbors as much as we love ourselves. This He called the second most important commandment. (See Mt 22:38.) If we see others being hurt, that love He commands might mean going to defend them—by fighting, if necessary, if the people attacking them refuse to listen and stop being mean. This is called the "Just War Tradition." It's lots of rules about how to use violence or force in a limited, *Christian* way.

(See next page.)

Review Session 2

1. The Reformation, we've learned, was a very important historical moment, when some brave Christians began reading their Bibles more carefully, in greater detail, and with deeper passion. Doing this led them (the Reformers) to rediscover theological truths like this: "We have been made right with God [justified] because of our faith. Now we have peace with Him because of our Lord Jesus Christ" (Rom 5:1). Who was the first champion of this statement? You might call him "the Father of the Reformation," the first Protestant.

    M _____ L _____

2. Fortunately for us, this man didn't keep this good news to himself; he shared it, like Jesus says we should. The people he shared it with did the same. Eventually, one such person, Andreas Osiander, shared it with an Englishman, Thomas Cranmer, who was the most important church leader in the kingdom of Henry VIII. In fact, Cranmer was the Archbishop of where?

    C _____

3. Having been converted to Protestantism, Cranmer wrote the Thirty-Nine Articles of Religion we've been studying. You can find them in the back of a *Book of Common Prayer*. They are a guide, a "shopping list" of essential, true statements about God, His son Jesus, and what their design/plan is for human life. Who is the other person of the Trinity? Do you know?

    (i) Tell me His name.

    The H _____

    (ii) On one occasion, He appeared in disguise as an animal. Draw that animal here.
    (Clue: He took this form at Christ's baptism in the Jordan River.)

4. God is a Trinity: three persons of one substance. Jesus, however, has two substances, which are combined in a hypostasis, a perfect unity. What are they?

H _____   D _____

5. Why does it even matter what we believe? Well, do you remember this diagram from Week 2? Fill in the blanks.

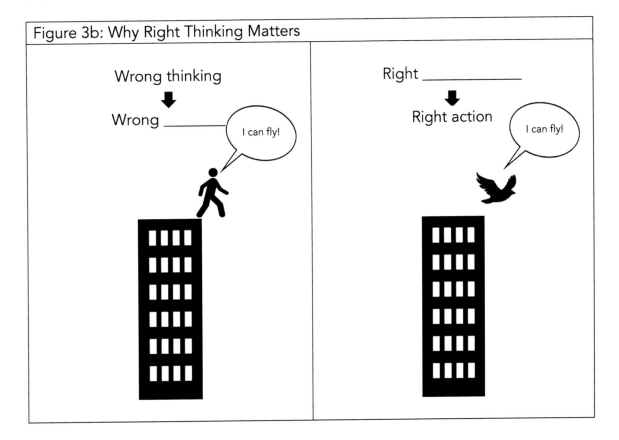

Figure 3b: Why Right Thinking Matters

Wrong thinking

Wrong _____   I can fly!

Right _____

Right action   I can fly!

SESSION 15

Article XXXVIII
Of Christian Men's Goods, Which Are Not Common

Do you remember in our discussion of Article XXXII when we heard how, in the early Church, the very first Christians shared with each other all of their belongings or possessions? These Cranmer calls our "goods." This is what he has to say about our "goods" in Article XXXVIII:

The riches and goods of Christians are not common, as touching the right, title, and possession of the same, as certain Anabaptists do falsely boast. Notwithstanding, every man ought, of such things as he possesseth, liberally to give alms to the poor, according to his ability.

To give "liberally," Cranmer means to give *generously*. Christians are supposed to give generously to those in need. Indeed, in (the gospel of) *Luke*, we hear John the Baptist teaching this rule of life: "'Anyone who has extra clothes should share with the one who has none.'" (See Lk 3:11.) That's hard. I (that is, Father Ben) have lots of coats. One is for summertime, which is really just to keep the rain off. The one for winter is warm, thick, and full of feathers—*mmm*. You know, I even have one I usually only wear to funerals (it's long and black). When you have too much of any one thing, it is called an "excess." You could say to me, therefore: "Father Ben, you have an excessive number of coats"—and you would be right! I also have an excess of shoes, shirts, books…*oh dear!* Having excessive material things is a sign of selfishness and of greed. And there are many people in the world who don't have enough of even the necessary (basic) things, like food and clean water. They would love to have just one of my many coats. God loves those people just as much as He loves me—*really*, He does.

Well, some Christians, therefore, and other people too, think that the right thing to do is to take away a person's excess and give it to those suffering a deficit (that's the opposite). Here, let me illustrate the meaning of these terms using the sundae glass from our discussion of Article XII:

Figure 12: Deficiency vs. Excess

Insufficient /
a "deficit"

Sufficient

More-than-sufficient / an
"excess" (too much!)

To take away anything from somebody else who doesn't agree to your doing that, *even* if that person has an excess, is robbery. Two wrongs don't make a right. Robin Hood, for example, was

a thief. His story might excite us, but would Jesus have pointed a bow and arrow in the face of bad guys? Or did He show bad guys how to live better lives by living one Himself: by being kind-hearted and forgiving and by living simply and being happy with what was sufficient? I think you know the answer. The Bible is clear—we just pretend it isn't.

Indeed, in the Reformation, when men and women started to read the Holy Scriptures again because it was available in their own languages, they rediscovered this truth about living simple lives for themselves. One group became famous for doing this very enthusiastically: the Anabaptists.

The Anabaptists first appeared in Zurich, Switzerland, listening to the rousing preaching of an early Reformation leader, Ulrich Zwingli. Their example of very visible, well-intentioned piety was copied by many others in nearby areas, such as in Austria. Here, a man called Jakob Hutter, a hatmaker, started a community that spread even to America; they were the Hutterites. (The Amish are another Anabaptist group that came here. You might have heard of them? They're probably the most famous Anabaptist group that still exists.)

In Germany, however, in the spring of 1534, some Anabaptists became deeply confused about the example of Christ, and seized control of the town of Münster. They walked up and down the streets with "axes, sledgehammers and long knives," broke into people's homes, and began redistributing their goods by force![36] This led to street battles between them and the locals, and those who resisted the robbers were murdered or forced to leave. Then, a combined army of Roman Catholics and Lutherans arrived to liberate Münster, and a long siege followed. For fourteen months, the Anabaptists resisted, but there was no hope. The liberators used a great many large cannons, and fired day after day against the walls and the gates. The people inside starved. They were desperate. Some even turned to cannibalism! Eventually, Münster was conquered. However, what happened there "shocked the whole of Europe."[37] It is perhaps with this terrible story in mind that Cranmer reminds us that "[t]he riches and goods of Christians are not common." They don't belong to everyone; they are an *individual*'s goods; they are *his* or *her* (private) property. They are another undeserved gift from God, yes, but a gift that God expects to be used as He would use it: for the pleasure and need of those with less, with "a deficit."

---

[36] Anthony Arthur, *The Tailor-King: The Rise and Fall of the Anabaptist Kingdom of Münster* (New York, NY: St. Martin's Press, 1999), 38.
[37] A.F. Pollard, *Thomas Cranmer and the English Reformation, 1489–1556* (New York, NY: G. P. Putnam's Sons, 1906), 123.

Article XXXIX
Of a Christian Man's Oath

As we confess that vain and rash swearing is forbidden Christian men by our Lord Jesus Christ, and James his Apostle, so we judge, that Christian Religion doth not prohibit, but that a man may swear when the magistrate requireth, in a cause of faith and charity, so it be done according to the prophet's teaching, in justice, judgement, and truth.

Cranmer isn't here talking about swearing as we might use that word, that is, being rude or "cussing." That's something the Bible tells us repeatedly not to do. (See Prov 4:24, 21:23; Eph 4:29, 5:4.) No, "to swear an oath" is to promise to do something. However, Cranmer here reminds us that, in the New Testament, we are cautioned about doing such a thing. James, Jesus's brother, for example, states that the problem with promising to do this or that is that we don't know what God will do between now and then. He writes,

> Now listen, you who say, "Today or tomorrow we will go to this or that city. We will spend a year there. We will buy and sell and make money." You don't even know what will happen tomorrow. What is your life? It is a mist that appears for a little while. Then it disappears. Instead, you should say, "If it pleases the LORD, we will live and do this or that." (Ja 4:13–15)

In other words, I might say to you, "I promise to see you on Sunday at church," but tonight, Jesus might come back. I don't know! After all, He did say that the General Resurrection and Day of Judgment would come suddenly. (See 1 Thess 5:1–3, for example.) I must, therefore, keep this in mind always. It's like I said when we looked at Article I: God doesn't just make everything; He also *keeps* it in existence. Every second, therefore, every breath, and every thought is one He has allowed us to have, so let us use those seconds, breaths, thoughts and everything else in *His* service. To Him be the glory forever and ever, amen.

Review Session 3

1. Do you remember the orange from the beginning of this course? I used it to illustrate the different ways that God communicates with us. The proper term is *revelation*. There are two types. Label this diagram.

Figure 2: ? vs. ?

Huh?

_____ Revelation

Here, this orange is for you.

_____ Revelation

2. The first kind of revelation is those truths about God we might glean from observing the natural world around us. The second way is more direct: it is those things that were too important to leave us guessing. He made an extra effort to let us know them, using at least three means.

    (i) A *very* special book. What is it?

    _____

    (ii) Chosen spokespeople under the influence of the Holy Spirit, like Jeremiah, were called

P _____

    (iii) An eternal Son, whose name is

J _____

3. Describe in your own words the Good News or Gospel.

    _____

    _____

    _____

    _____

    _____

BIBLIOGRAPHY

"Archbishop of Canterbury Receives the Coronation Bible at Lambeth Palace." *The Archbishop of Canterbury*. Posted April 20, 2023. Available at https://www.archbishopofcanterbury. org/news/ news-and-statements/archbishop-canterbury-receives-coronation-bible-lambeth- palace#:~:text=When%20the%201953%20Coronation%20Bible,the%20lively%20 Oracles%20of%20God.%E2%80%9D.

Alighieri, Dante. *The Divine Comedy of Dante Alighieri: Volume 2: Purgatorio*. Edited by Robert M. Durling. Oxford, UK: Oxford University Press, 2003.

Arthur, Anthony. *The Tailor-King: The Rise and Fall of the Anabaptist Kingdom of Muenster*. New York, NY: St. Martin's Press, 1999.

Backus, Irena. *Leibniz: Protestant Theologian*. Oxford; New York, NY: Oxford University Press, 2016.

Bass, Justin W. *The Battle for the Keys: Revelation 1:18 and Christ's Descent into the Underworld*. Milton Keynes, UK: Paternoster, 2014.

Beer, Barrett L. *Rebellion and Riot: Popular Disorder in England During the Reign of Edward VI*. Kent, OH: The Kent State University Press, 2005.

Bray, Gerald. *The Faith We Confess: An Exposition of the Thirty-Nine Articles*. London: The Latimer Trust, 2009.

Brooks, Peter. "The Theology of Thomas Cranmer." In *The Cambridge Companion to Reformation Theology*. Edited by David Bagchi & David C. Steinmetz, pp. 150-160. Cambridge (UK): Cambridge University Press, 2004.

——— . *Thomas Cranmer's Doctrine of the Eucharist: An Essay in Historical Development*. London: MacMillan & Co., Ltd., 1965.

Buchanan, Colin. *A Case for Infant Baptism*. Cambridge, UK: Grove Books, Ltd., 2009.

Burk, Denny. "Was the Apostle Paul Married?" Available at https://www.dennyburk.com/was-the-apostle-paul-married/, (accessed May 1, 2024).

Collins, Kenneth J. *A Real Christian: The Life of John Wesley*. Nashville, TN: Abingdon Press, 1999.

Couenhoven, Jesse. "St. Augustine's Doctrine of Original Sin." *Augustinian Studies* 36, No. 2 (2005): pp. 359-396.

Craig, William Lane. *Atonement and the Death of Christ: An Exegetical, Historical, and Philosophical Exploration.* Waco, TX: Baylor University Press, 2020.

Cummings, Brian. "Introduction." *The Book of Common Prayer: The Texts of 1549, 1559, and 1662.* Oxford, UK: Oxford University Press, 2011: ix–lii.

Davie, Martin. *Our Inheritance of Faith: A Commentary on the Thirty-Nine Articles.* West Knapton, UK: Gilead Books Publishing, 2019.

———. *The Gospel and the Anglican Tradition.* West Knapton, UK: Gilead Books Publishing, 2018.

Edwards, Jonathan. *Heaven Is a World of Love.* Wheaton, IL: Crossway, 2020.

Emerson, Matthew Y. *"He Descended To the Dead": An Evangelical Theology of Holy Saturday.* Downers Grove, IL: InterVarsity Press, 2019.

Gäbler, Ulrich. *Huldrych Zwingli: His Life and Work.* Translated by Ruth C. L. Gritsch. Philadelphia, PA: Fortress Press, 1986.

Gospel Coalition, The, Redeemer Presbyterian Church, and Kathy Keller. *The New City Catechism: 52 Questions and Answers for our Hearts and Minds.* Wheaton, IL: Crossway, 2017.

Gospel Coalition, The. *The New City Catechism: Curriculum—Volume 3: Spirit, Restoration, Growing in Grace.* Wheaton, IL: Crossway, 2018.

Hall, Basil. "Martin Bucer in England." In *Martin Bucer: Reforming Church and Community.* Edited by D. F. Wright, pp. 144-160. Cambridge (UK): Cambridge University Press, 1994.

Hopf, Constantin. *Martin Bucer and the English Reformation.* Eugene, OR: Wipf and Stock Publishers, 2012.

Leibniz, Gottfried Wilhelm. *Philosophical Papers and Letters: Volume II.* Translated by Leroy E. Loemker. Chicago, IL: The University of Chicago Press, 1956.

Lewis, C. S. *The Silver Chair.* New York, NY: HarperTrophy: 1981.

Lillback, Peter A. "The Early Reformed Covenant Paradigm: Vermigli in the Context of Bullinger, Luther and Calvin." In *Peter Martyr Vermigli & the European Reformations: Semper Reformanda.* Edited by Frank A. James III, pp. 70-96. Leiden, The Netherlands; Boston, MA: Koninklijke Brill NV, 2004.

MacCulloch, Diarmaid. *The Reformation: A History,* New York, NY: Viking, 2004.

———. *Thomas Cranmer: A Life.* New Haven, CT: Yale University Press, 1996.

MacCulloch, J. A. *The Harrowing of Hell: A Comparative Study of an Early Christian Doctrine*. Edinburgh: T. & T. Clark, 1930.

Machowski, Marty. *The Ology: Ancient Truths Ever New*. Greensboro, NC: New Growth Press, 2015.

McArthur, Harvey. "Celibacy in Judaism at the Time of Christian Beginnings." *Andrews University Seminary Studies* 25, No. 2 (1987): pp. 163-181.

McGrath, Alister E. *Theology: The Basics*. Chichester, UK; Hoboken, NJ: John Wiley & Sons Ltd., 2018.

Morris, Leon. *The Atonement: Its Meaning & Significance*. Downers Grove, IL: InterVarsity Press, 1983.

Neelands, David. "Predestination and the *Thirty-Nine Articles*." In *A Companion to Peter Martyr Vermigli*. Edited by Torrance Kirby, pp. 355-374. Leiden, The Netherlands; Boston, MA: Koninklijke Brill NV, 2009.

Null, Ashley. "Conversion to Communion: Thomas Cranmer on a Favourite Puritan Theme." *The Churchman* 116, No. 3 (2002): pp. 239-257.

———. *Thomas Cranmer's Doctrine of Repentance: Renewing the Power to Love*. Oxford: Oxford University Press, 2000.

O'Donovan, Oliver. *On the Thirty-Nine Articles: A Conversation with Tudor Christianity*. London: SCM Press, 2011.

Ozment, Steven. *The Age of Reform, 1250-1550: An Intellectual and Religious History of Late Medieval and Reformation Europe*. New Haven, CT: Yale University Press, 2020.

Packer, J. I. *I Want to be a Christian*. Wheaton, IL: Tyndale House Publishers, 1977.

Phipps, William E. *Clerical Celibacy: The Heritage*. New York, NY: The Continuum International Publishing Group, 2004.

Piper, John. *The Pleasures of God: Meditations on God's Delight in Being God*. Portland, OR: Multnomah Books, 1991.

Pollard, A.F. *Thomas Cranmer and the English Reformation, 1489–1556*. New York, NY: G.P. Putnam's Sons, 1906.

Rodgers, John H. *Essential Truths for Christians: A Commentary on the Anglican Thirty-Nine Articles and an Introduction to Systematic Theology*. Blue Bell, PA: Classical Anglican Press, 2011.

Stott, John R. W. *The Cross of Christ: 20th Anniversary Edition*. Downers Grove, IL: InterVarsity Press, 2006.

Strickland, Lloyd. *Leibniz Reinterpreted*. London; New York, NY: Continuum International Publishing Group, 2006.

Tertullian. "On the Flesh of Christ." *Christian Classics Ethereal Library*. Accessed November 7, 2023. https://ccel.org/ccel/tertullian/christ flesh/anf03.v.vii.i.html.

The Book of Common Prayer and Administration of the Sacraments and Other Rites and Ceremonies of the Church together with The Psalter or Psalms of David According to the use of The Episcopal Church. New York, NY: Church Publishing Inc., 2007.

Torrance, Thomas F. *Atonement*. Downers Grove, IL: IVP Academic, 2009.

——— . "Predestination in Christ." *The Evangelical Quarterly* 13, No. 2 (April 1941): pp. 108-141.

Tozer, A. W. *God's Pursuit of Man*. Chicago, IL: Moody Publishers, 1978.

Williams, Leslie. *Emblem of Faith Untouched: A Short Life of Thomas Cranmer*. Grand Rapids, MI: Wm. B. Eerdmans Publishing Company, 2016.

Wilson, Douglas. *To a Thousand Generations: Infant Baptism—Covenant Mercy for the People of God*. Moscow, ID: Canon Press, 1996.

Wright, N. T. "Rethinking the Tradition." In *For All the Saints? Remembering the Christian Departed*. Edited by N. T. Wright, pp. 20-46. London: SPCK, 2003.

Wright, Tom. *Justification: God's Plan and Paul's* Vision, London: SPCK, 2009.

——— . *What Saint Paul Really Said*. Oxford, UK: Lion, 1997.